DEPARTMENT OF THE ARMY HISTORICAL SUMMARY

DEPARTMENT
OF THE
ARMY HISTORICAL SUMMARY

FISCAL YEAR 1969

COMPILED AND EDITED

BY

WILLIAM GARDNER BELL

GOVERNMENT REPRINTS PRESS
Washington, D.C.

© Ross & Perry, Inc. 2002 on new material. All rights reserved.

No claim to U.S. government work contained throughout this book.

Protected under the Berne Convention.

Printed in The United States of America
Ross & Perry, Inc. Publishers
216 G St., N.E.,
Washington, D.C. 20002
Telephone (202) 675-8300
Facsimile (801)459-7535
info@RossPerry.com

SAN 253-8555

Government Reprints Press Edition 2002

Government Reprints Press is an Imprint of Ross & Perry, Inc.

Library of Congress Control Number: 2001096861
http://www.GPOreprints.com

ISBN 1-931839-35-2

Book Cover designed by Sapna. sapna@rossperry.com

⊗ The paper used in this publication meets the requirements for permanence established by
the American National Standard for Information Sciences "Permanence of Paper for Printed
Library Materials" (ANSI Z39.48-1984).

Foreword

Annual accounts of Army expenditures, work, and accomplishments have been published since 1822. Those prepared prior to that date, starting with Secretary of War Henry Knox's report of 1792, were published in 1832 in the military affairs volumes of *American State Papers*. In the World War II period, under the pressures of wartime conditions, the traditional report was suspended after publication of the fiscal year 1941 edition, and was resumed with a 17-month edition spanning the period July 1947–November 1948, nominally the fiscal year 1948 report. (The six-year gap between July 1941 and June 1947 was bridged in part by biennial reports of the Under Secretary of the Army and the Chief of Staff.) At that juncture, following creation in 1947 of the National Military Establishment, the Army Secretary's report became a part of the Semi-Annual Report of the Secretary of Defense, beginning with the July–December 1949 edition. The annual frequency was then resumed, and the reports of the Secretary of Defense and the three service secretaries appeared in a consolidated document for two decades.

In May 1972 the Annual Report of the Department of Defense was canceled. The last consolidated report to be published was that of fiscal year 1968. Because of the unique nature and long standing of the Army report, and especially because of its demonstrated value as a reference document—in effect, the Army's memory—the Army decided to continue publication separately under a title of departmental complexion. Publication is resumed with this, the fiscal year 1969 edition.

Washington, D.C.

JAMES L. COLLINS, JR.
Brigadier General, USA
Chief of Military History

Contents

I. Introduction

While the Vietnam War remained the dominant factor in Army affairs during fiscal year 1969, the closing month of the year brought a milestone in the conflict when President Richard M. Nixon, meeting with the Republic of Vietnam's President Nguyen Van Thieu on Midway Island in the Pacific, announced on June 8 that 25,000 American troops would be withdrawn from the war zone by the end of August 1969.

This first redeployment of American forces—made possible by an extended U.S. effort to arm, equip, and train Republic of Vietnam forces to assume an expanding role on the battlefield—will include Army and other service elements heavily weighted with combat troops and roughly equivalent to a division force. The first major Army units to be pulled out will be two brigades of the 9th Infantry Division.

The reduction follows a year during which strength in Vietnam remained relatively constant at about 350,000 of the Army's million-and-a-half personnel. Unit deployment was also stable, with $8\frac{1}{3}$ of the Army's $19\frac{2}{3}$ division force equivalents (18 numbered divisions plus 5 independent brigades comprising a $1\frac{2}{3}$ division force equivalent) still on station in the combat theater.

Active and relatively sustained operations throughout the year produced high casualties. Of the 11,338 American battle deaths in the 12-month period, the Army lost 7,653. Of the 77,391 Americans wounded by hostile action in the period, 53,034 were Army personnel, of whom more than 30,000 were returned to duty without requiring hospital care. On the last day of March 1969, the number of American battle deaths surpassed the losses (33,629) sustained in the Korean War. The Vietnam War thus became the fourth costliest—after the Civil War and the two World Wars—in our history. Over the full course of our involvement, from January 1961 through June 1969, 36,954 Americans have died and 237,024 were wounded as a result of hostile action.

During fiscal year 1969 the Army reached its highest strength since the Korean War and operated on its highest budget since World War II. An average of 30,000 men were trained and shipped to Vietnam each month, while sizable forces in Europe and Korea were sustained and the Strategic Reserve in the United States was maintained in a state of readiness despite the turbulent conditions generated by oversea requirements.

The extent of this achievement is revealed in some of the details of the Army's personnel situation in fiscal year 1969. Of the more than 1.5 million men and women in the Army, about 700,000 were serving overseas, many in short tour areas. Close to a complete replacement was required for the more than 350,000 in Vietnam. Not all of the approximately 800,000 Army members in the United States could be applied to the rotation base; 197,000 were trainees not ready for assignment. The problem was to balance grades and skills worldwide and administer short and long tour schedules equitably with $10\frac{1}{3}$ division forces in short tour areas and $9\frac{1}{3}$ in long tour areas. The difficulty of maintaining balance, achieving stability, insuring readiness, and preserving equity is readily apparent. Understandably, the monumental demands led to some deterioration in readiness, imbalances in the distribution of skills, involuntary personnel assignments, and dislocation of rotational patterns. Yet it is unlikely that any service of any nation ever structured such an equitable system and came as close to carrying it out. That it was accomplished is a tribute to efficient and effective management and control at all levels throughout the Army.

Military management has become increasingly formal, technical, and universal in recent years. The Army has taken advantage of new technology and techniques in the management field to insure that those who make decisions and those who carry them out have the comprehensive, accurate, and timely information that is required to administer a military service in modern times. Over the past several years Army management procedures and controls have been strengthened; management organizational patterns have been simplified and streamlined; the use of computer technology has been expanded; new management systems and techniques have been introduced; and the total management effort has been centralized at the top levels of the departmental staff. In the past year the Computer Systems Command was established to integrate the automatic data processing effort and insure its responsiveness to the Army's worldwide needs. The Army Authorization Documents System was completed in the fall of 1968, providing a data bank to record equipment and personnel requirements for each of 20,000 units identified under the Force Accounting System, which has been operating since mid-1967. All of these management innovations and refinements made it possible for the Army to meet more effectively such diverse national responsibilities as fighting a war in Asia, coping with civil disturbances at home, and developing a ballistic missile defense system against possible future need.

Some of the problems associated with these responsibilities are beyond the scope of military management and transcended the realm of military control, while at the same time they have had a broad impact on military operation. The Vietnam War, civil rights, and weapons systems development have created social unrest of concern to the Army as well as to other institutions and activities in American society. The agitation—some of it evolutionary, some revolutionary—has ranged from disagreement and resistance to disobedience and confrontation, and all of it has had a bearing on military interests, responsibilities, and operations.

Since American participation in the Vietnam War has been founded on an ideological premise rather than on territorial threat, and has required only selective manpower levies and partial mobilization, the conscription process has been marred by draft evasion and card burning. A fugitive colony in Canada, the occasional public destruction of an official document, and attempts to disrupt recruiting activities have been widely reported, along with some in-service dissent by several antiwar groups and individuals and the defection to Sweden of a small band of dissidents. Inescapably, these activities affect the acquisition of manpower, the development of effective forces, and the maintenance of morale both on and off the battlefield. It has been suggested that these problems could be eliminated by the creation of an all-volunteer Army. Whether such a force would be practicable and attainable is being studied by the Army as well as by a presidential commission.

The recently developed campus opposition to the Reserve Officers' Training Corps program is another area of Army concern. A primary source of commissioned leaders for the active Army, the ROTC program produced over 16,000 officers in fiscal year 1969. The importance of the program is illustrated by a few examples. At one point in the year there were 155 Army general officers on active duty who started their careers as ROTC cadets. At other points during the year the Deputy Commanding General, both Field Force commanders, and five division commanders in Vietnam were officers commissioned through ROTC. The same was also true of the Army's Assistant Vice Chief of Staff and the principal military adviser to our negotiating team in Paris. The scope of military service today is broad, and the ROTC program permits the matriculation of educated Americans from all backgrounds and regions in the land, to the obvious benefit of the institution and the nation they will serve. It is clearly in the national interest that the ROTC program be continued.

The advancement of civil rights and the development of weapons systems are also national concerns that involve social, political, and military considerations and heavy Army commitment. In the field of civil rights the military services have long set standards of equal treatment and opportunity for all personnel, and while on the home front we still have a long way to go to match, for example, the celebrated racial compatibility of the battlefield, progress is being made. In the last year there was notable advance in the active program to insure equal opportunity for minority groups in off-post housing.

It has not been possible for all of the Army's efforts to be along such productive lines. Unfortunately, the impulse for further civil rights progress has led, in its most acute form, to civil disturbances requiring the use of troops to support civil authorities, the development of an organizational structure and plans to deal with emergencies, the institution of riot control training for troop units, the regional positioning of emergency equipment against need, and the diversion of military manpower and funds from other purposes. As long as there is a need (and there has been at various times and for various reasons throughout our history), just so long will the Army have to be prepared to act in controlling civil disturbances.

In modern times the development of strategic weapons systems, both offensive and defensive, is influenced by such considerations as national defense, the international balance of power, the state of the art, the availability of funds, national priorities, and the consent of both the Congress and the governed. As in all areas of human affairs, there is little likelihood of complete agreement on the social, political, and military factors involved in such a highly technical and complex field. The nation's experience with an antiballistic missile system is a case in point.

The Army's Sentinel ballistic missile defense system, an evolution from the NIKE-X, was conceived as a limited one that would provide area protection of U.S. population centers against a Chinese attack, and offer an option to counter a larger Soviet threat should that develop. Initial survey work near some major cities produced opposition by local groups toward the end of 1968. President Nixon, shortly after taking office early in 1969, designated the system as Safeguard and redefined its objectives; it was to be a purely defensive measure against a threat to our retaliatory forces, a threat from Red China in the next decade, or an accidental or irrational attack from any source. Despite this redirection, the Safeguard system was the center of active debate in and out of government up to the close of the fiscal year, the differences revolving around feasibility, cost, and arms race considerations. The outcome will proceed from congressional action on the program in the coming fiscal year.

From the foregoing it is evident that there have been problems as well as accomplishments connected with the Army's operation over the past year. Despite the appearances of dissent, facing the problems has revealed the readiness of the vast majority of citizens and soldiers to accept civic responsibility and meet the obligations of service. Where performance of duty is concerned, the American soldier today is proving himself equal if not superior to his predecessor of any generation. The quality of Army personnel—civilian and military, at home and abroad, in or out of combat—is reflected in the worldwide efficiency and effectiveness of the Army during the report period. Further highlights and details of the year's operation are set forth in the following pages.

II. Operational Readiness

The Army's operational mission involves the readiness, deployment, and utilization of U.S. ground forces. To carry it out the Army must develop strategic concepts and plans, insure the operational readiness of forces, establish priorities for their distribution worldwide, and supervise their commitment in support of national policies. In fiscal year 1969 this over-all task was shaped by the Army's million-and-a-half strength, its heavy contribution to the war in Vietnam, and its worldwide deployment.

The Pacific and the Far East

The area of the U.S. Army, Pacific, embraces Hawaii, Korea, and Southeast Asia. Command strength continued to rise as a result of the war. During the year, operational forces in the Pacific reached a level of nine combat divisions, six combat units of brigade size, five corps or equivalent headquarters, and a multitude of support elements ranging from a missile command and air defense brigades in Korea to engineer, military police, signal, and aviation brigades in Vietnam.

Army strength in Vietnam rose during fiscal year 1969 from 355,000 to about 361,000. Deployed to the combat theater were the 1st Brigade of the 5th Infantry Division (Mechanized), four artillery battalions, an aviation battalion, and numerous support units. Forty-three Reserve Component units, including two artillery battalions, an engineer battalion, a ranger company, and various combat service support units, were deployed to Vietnam during the period June–December 1968. Within the combat zone, an additional corps headquarters, the XXIV, was activated in August 1968 to facilitate command and control of forces in the Republic of Vietnam's northern provinces. At the divisional level, the 101st Airborne Division was reorganized into an airmobile division, the second of its type in the U.S. Army; the 23d Infantry Division (American) was restructured along the lines of the other infantry divisions in Vietnam, its three brigades—the 11th, 196th, and 198th—retaining their numerical designation; and the 9th Infantry Division was reorganized so that one brigade achieved a riverine configuration.

The Army's standardization program, designed to provide more firepower and improved combat effectiveness, was extended in the war zone to combat support units and was in the process, as the year closed, of being extended to combat service support units to foster economies in critical personnel skills and materiel.

On the battlefield, U.S. Army forces operated in all areas of the Republic of Vietnam during the fiscal year and in three major roles: containment operations along the demilitarized zone and the Cambodian and Laotian borders to prevent enemy incursions into South Vietnam; offensive operations against enemy main forces and their base areas; and support operations to further the Republic of Vietnam's pacification program. Offensive and containment operations constituted the primary roles. These operations compelled the enemy to rely heavily on border sanctuaries and kept the bulk of his main forces away from population centers, while pacification activities furthered population security and helped the Republic of Vietnam government extend its protection into new rural areas.

Friendly forces maintained the initiative over enemy main forces, capitalizing on superior firepower and mobility. Wide-ranging spoiling attacks, capture of supply caches, and penetrations of base areas kept the enemy off balance, although he continued to demonstrate an ability to mount co-ordinated countrywide attacks. His casualties continued to run substantially above those of the allies.

Increasing enemy concentration in the areas west and north of Saigon necessitated a readjustment of friendly forces. Reduced activity in the I Corps area in the north permitted the shift of some elements to the threatened area. To the south of the capital city, an Army-Navy team continued to conduct operations along the many waterways in the Mekong Delta. Mobile riverine forces penetrated areas previously thought to be inaccessible, denying the enemy important sanctuaries and helping to restore government control over an important food-producing region.

The Army was also deeply involved in the program to improve and modernize the Republic of Vietnam armed forces, preparing them to assume an expanding and eventually a major share of the war. Issue of the M–16 rifle and the M–60 machine gun enhanced the confidence, morale, and effectiveness of the Vietnamese forces. Army advisory teams in all 44 of the country's provinces concentrated on improving the Republic of Vietnam Army and Regional and Popular Forces units. The over-all expansion of indigenous armed forces aims at a balanced structure of combat and logistical units capable of coping with insurgents.

As the year ended there were important indications, on several levels, of progress in the modernization program, the war, and U.S. participation. It was possible, first of all, to reduce the number of advisers assigned to some of the regular Republic of Vietnam Army units. Secondly, those units were able to assume an expanding role in independent operations. And finally, the President of the United States in the closing month of the year announced an early withdrawal of some U.S. troops, the first force reduction of the war.

An 11,000-man division of Thai Army troops completed its deployment to Vietnam early in calendar year 1969, moving to bases in the III Corps Tactical Zone and replacing a previously committed Thai regiment. The U.S. Army advisory contingent—instructors, logisticians, repairmen—that helped prepare the division for Vietnam was phased out as the fiscal year closed. The Thai Army will train the division's replacements at the Kanchanaburi training center in Thailand, built by the U.S. Army.

Communist insurgency in Thailand continued during 1969, especially among hill tribes in the north. Government counterinsurgency programs progressed slowly but steadily in the northeastern and central regions of the country.

In Korea, the U.S. commitment continued, with Eighth Army elements deployed along the demilitarized zone (DMZ) with Republic of Korea forces. The I Corps (Group), the 2d and 7th Infantry Divisions, the 4th Missile Command, and the 38th Artillery Brigade (Air Defense) joined Republic of Korea Army forces in measures to defend the nation. The I Corps defended the western avenues of approach into South Korea with the 2d Infantry Division deployed along the DMZ and the 7th Infantry Division in reserve. Units regularly conducted combat training and held frequent exercises to test and maintain combat readiness, while the U.S. Military Advisory Group helped the Republic of Korea's Army to develop and maintain its forces.

Hostile actions by North Korea along the DMZ and elsewhere in the Republic of Korea continued as a part of the long-term objective of reunifying Korea under Communist rule. A high proportion of provocations has been directed against the U.S. 2d Division, apparently part of a deliberate attempt to bolster North Korean claims that DMZ tension is attributable to the presence of U.S. forces.

Elsewhere in the Far East–Pacific region, U.S. Army deployment in Japan and on Okinawa remained generally stable. On Okinawa, in addition to Headquarters, U.S. Army, Ryukyu Islands, and Headquarters, IX Corps, the principal Army forces consisted of the 2d Logistical Command, the 30th Artillery Brigade (Air Defense), the 7th Psychological Operations Group, the 1st Special Forces Group, and the 97th Civil Affairs Group.

In Japan, the U.S. Army headquarters at Camp Zama continued to provide logistical support to U.S. and allied forces in the Far East, including military assistance, depot operations, procurement, and hospital facilities. The command operated 2,750 hospital beds for battle casualties from Vietnam.

Europe, the Middle East, and Africa

U.S. Army, Europe, maintains a powerful armored-mechanized nuclear-supported force that is a keystone of North Atlantic Treaty Organization land defense in central Europe. Among the major forces are 2 armored divisions, 2⅓ mechanized infantry divisions, and 2 armored cavalry regiments. Support includes nuclear-capable artillery units.

In December 1968 the Secretary of Defense approved an Army plan to streamline the command, control, and logistic organization of Army forces in Europe. As the fiscal year closed, changes were in progress to replace the 7th Army Support Command with two corps support commands, redesignate the Communications Zone as the Theater Army Support Command, establish a single automated inventory control center for the theater, and streamline command relationships with NATO.

The redeployment of Army units from Europe, begun in April 1968, was completed in September 1968 under a plan that reduced Army strength there by about 28,000 men. The two brigades of the 24th Infantry Division (Mechanized), the 3d Armored Cavalry, and combat and service support units returned to the United States remain committed to NATO, and selected organizational equipment was stored upon their departure against a time of future need. With this equipment prepositioned, the units can be flown to the theater and take the field expeditiously in a period of crisis. To test the procedure, over 12,000 of these troops were flown back to Germany to participate, during January and February 1969, in Exercise Reforger. A successful operation with realistic training under winter conditions, the exercise took on added significance in the light of developments in Eastern Europe during the period.

Under the guise of military "exercises," the armed forces of the Warsaw Pact nations invaded Czechoslovakia on August 20, 1968. Their deployment placed large and mobile Soviet forces farther to the west than at any time in recent years, placed Soviet divisions closer to U.S. Army forces, and in general altered the military balance in Europe. The forward positioning of Soviet forces with the corresponding extension of their lines of communication significantly improved their ability to attack with little or no warning.

The rapidity and secrecy with which the Warsaw Pact forces deployed brings into challenge the premise that there would be sufficient time to mobilize and deploy large ground forces; the advantages of having forces in being and deployed according to plan are obvious.

The United States, in concert with its NATO allies, responded to the Czechoslovakian situation by taking measures to improve the treaty organization's military posture. The NATO ministers, meeting in November 1968, affirmed that the "quality, effectiveness, and deployment" of NATO forces would be improved. In response to the Czechoslovakian crisis and as a display of the U.S. Army's deployment capability, the timetable for Exercise Reforger was accelerated. Additional resources were also allocated to European-based elements and those scheduled to reinforce them in order to raise the level of preparedness.

During fiscal year 1969 the United States and Spain negotiated for a renewal of the agreement under which U.S. armed forces are granted base rights on Spanish territory. United States use of these bases assumed increased importance as a result of France's military withdrawal from NATO and the growing Soviet naval presence in the Mediterranean. The U.S. Army's modest participation in the base rights agreement consists chiefly of military assistance grants and sales designed to improve the capabilities of the Spanish Army.

Alaska and Latin America

The U.S. Army, Alaska, continued as the Army component of the unified Alaskan Command charged with providing Alaska's ground defense. The tactical forces are positioned in two general locations—about half are north of the Alaskan Range in the Fort Wainwright–Eielson Air Force Base complex near Fairbanks and are assigned to or support the 171st Mechanized Infantry Brigade; the remainder are in the Fort Richardson–Elmendorf Air Force Base complex near Anchorage in the south, where they are assigned to or support the 172d Mechanized Infantry Brigade. Each brigade has two maneuver battalions and a battalion of artillery.

Alaska affords a fine natural training area with virgin land, muskeg, woods, mountains, lakes and rivers, and cold weather. The wide variety and range of geographic and meteorological conditions contributes to the development of well-conditioned and versatile forces. Two Alaskan-trained infantry battalions sent to Vietnam were rated among the best-prepared units to enter the war there, despite environmental differences.

Headquartered in the Panama Canal Zone, the U.S. Army Forces, Southern Command, continued as the Army component of the unified U.S. Southern Command. The 193d Infantry Brigade was the major tactical unit, with organic mechanized and infantry battalions, a field artillery battery, an engineer company, and an aviation company. Other units include the 8th Special Forces Group (Airborne), the 4th Missile Battalion of the 517th Artillery, the 470th Intelligence Group, the 3d Civil Affairs Group, the U.S. Army School of the Americas, the Inter-American Geodetic Survey, and the Atlantic Area Installation Command. Command of all active elements of U.S. Army Forces, Southern Command, in Puerto Rico is scheduled to be transferred to the U.S. Continental Army Command and administered by Third U.S. Army effective July 1, 1969. All preparations for this transfer of responsibility were accomplished within the fiscal year.

The Southern Command's functions are varied, ranging from actual participation in the defense and security of U.S. personnel and property in the Canal Zone to assistance to Latin American countries engaged in counterinsurgency operations. Through the U.S. Army School of the Americas, mobile training teams, and Army sections of military groups in 17 countries, U.S. Army personnel provided valuable guidance and professional military assistance and advice to the armed forces of Latin American nations.

Continental United States

The U.S. Army Air Defense Command, a component of the combined U.S.-Canadian Air Defense Force, is the Army's only continental U.S. command assigned an operational alert mission and deployed on tactical sites. The command's six air defense brigades and eight groups, with NIKE–HERCULES and HAWK fire units, defend 25 industrial and population centers in 14 states on a 24-hour-a-day basis.

During fiscal year 1969 all Air Defense Command units met prescribed training requirements, and 72 percent attained the highest possible rating for mission performance. Improved operational capability was confirmed in the annual service practice missile firing at Fort Bliss, Texas, and by generally higher unit scores earned in tactical evaluations.

There were several reductions in antibomber and area defenses during the year. Thirteen NIKE–HERCULES fire units and 2 headquarters were inactivated in the first half of the fiscal year and another 17 fire units and 5 headquarters were scheduled for inactivation and declared nonoperational by year-end.

Army Readiness

The continuing program to improve the Army's readiness has proceeded concurrently with and been conditioned by the over-all buildup, the war, and the modernization program for Vietnamese forces. The status of major units improved slightly during the year as the result of close management of their personnel, training, and equipment. There was some decline in the readiness of support units, both in the active Army and the Reserve Components, because of war requirements. Diversions of equipment from active Army and Reserve Component units, delays in planned replacements, and levies on war reserve stocks were necessary to meet the expanding requirements connected with Vietnamese force improvement and modernization.

With the leveling off of the U.S. Army commitment in Vietnam, marked by the last scheduled deployment of a maneuver battalion in July 1968, and the anticipated assumption by Vietnamese forces of an increasing role on the battlefield, attention turned to the considerations of stabilization and, in the longer view, redeployment. The Strategic Army Force (STRAF) was strengthened with the activation and assignment to the 82d Airborne Division of a brigade to replace the one deployed to Vietnam. The STRAF was thus enlarged to 4⅓ divisions. The 76 mobilized Reserve Component units completed their training and 43 were deployed to Southeast Asia and 33 assigned to the STRAF as operationally ready units. The assignment of combat veterans to elements of the Strategic Reserve enhanced readiness, and the adjustment in Vietnam also had a calming effect on personnel turbulence in U.S. Army, Europe.

In June 1969 the Army operations center (AOC) was moved into a new facility in the basement of the Pentagon. The new complex houses all of the elements of the center, including the U.S. Army Command and Control Support Detachment and the Civil Disturbance Watch Team of the Directorate for Civil Disturbance Planning and Operations. Parts of the AOC were formerly spread throughout the Pentagon and in other external locations. The consolidation will provide a capability for more effective, efficient, and timely crisis management at departmental headquarters. Improved communications provide more flexibility for coping with both domestic and international crises.

The AOC was the hub of staff activity on four separate occasions in fiscal year 1969. In the presidential election campaign of 1968 the center's co-ordinated Army resources supporting the Secret Service in its role of protecting the President and Vice President of the United States and all candidates for those offices, right through to completion of the inaugural ceremonies. The Army provided explosive ordnance disposal personnel, regular troop units (see below), helicopters, radios, sentry dog teams, and other kinds of equipment and personnel.

In a worldwide command post exercise in October 1968, the AOC provided essential command, control, and administrative direction for the Army Staff during exercise play.

The coup d'etat in Panama in October 1968 produced an international situation in which the center supported the Army Staff with accurate and current information through briefings, maps, charts, and other displays.

On the domestic scene, the Army operations center during the winter and early spring of 1969 monitored the military assistance provided to civil authorities in connection with disastrous floods in southern California and the northern states of the Midwest. Beginning in late February 1969, the center was the Department of Defense focal point for military participation in Operation Forecast, a massive flood prevention effort co-ordinated by the Office of Emergency Preparedness.

In the past year the Operations Center System almost doubled the size of its data base, adding several new reporting systems and related files. The most significant of these are the Unit Identification Code Registration and Deployment Reporting System. These and other information systems required the augmentation of center equipment.

The Deployment Reporting System has opened an entirely new area in the processes of planning and analysis. The system is designed to provide information required for contingency planning, mobility planning, strategic studies, feasibility estimates, operational plan package reviews, and movement capability studies. It was initiated as a joint planning automatic data processing system in March 1969 and when fully operational will permit rapid evaluation of operational plans and the Army's capability to execute them.

Civil Disturbances

In anticipation of civil disturbances during the Democratic National Convention in August 1968, an active Army task force of three brigades, totaling 6,277 troops, was prepositioned on August 26 in the Chicago, Illinois, area, to be available on call. The force was not used and by August 30 began returning to home stations. The estimated cost of the operation was $1.324 million. Unlike 1968, federal troops were not required in fiscal year 1969 to assist civil authorities in situations of civil disturbance. In response to 35 requests, riot control materiel such as protective masks and vests, CS grenades, and communications equipment was loaned to civil law enforcement agencies and National Guard elements from 12 states and the District of Columbia.

Despite the quieter year, plans for possible disturbances in the 50 states, the District of Columbia, Puerto Rico, and other possessions or territories were completed and co-ordinated with the jurisdictions and the other military services, and civil disturbance training was conducted by all Army components.

Civil Affairs, Civic Action, Psychological Operations, and Special Forces

The major civil affairs and civic action commitments and responsibilities in oversea areas remained in Southeast Asia and Latin America during fiscal year 1969. In Vietnam, the U.S. Army continued to support that country's pacification program. The Office of Civil Operations and Revolutionary Development Support (CORDS) of the Military

Assistance Command provided single manager direction over all U.S. civil and military support there.

CORDS supports activities that promote security in villages and hamlets, neutralization of the Viet Cong infrastructure, defection by the enemy, care and resettlement of refugees, and community organization and self-government. CORDS agencies are engaged in programs to improve agriculture, education, and medical care; public safety; road and utilities systems; facilities of various kinds; and numerous other civic enterprises to promote the welfare of the people and repair the ravages of war.

Army civil affairs units and civic action support contributed to the over-all pacification program. Three civil affairs companies and four platoons operated in the field during the year, chiefly at province and district levels, conducting water surveys, hiring laborers, providing medical and dental care, rendering assistance to refugees, constructing schools and sanitary facilities, and providing agricultural and foreign claims advice.

Eight military surgical teams worked in provincial hospitals, supporting the Republic of Vietnam Ministry of Public Health by providing medical care for civilians; furnishing advice and assistance in public health and sanitation; and training Vietnamese personnel in medical care, public health, and sanitation. Two engineer construction advisory detachments supported the Vietnamese government's rural development program, one providing assistance in repairing dwellings and constructing roads, schools, and dispensaries, the other in constructing water systems. The detachments also provided the rural population with technical assistance in well-drilling, sewer construction, and construction techniques for self-help projects.

Senior U.S. Army advisers, specially selected and trained, worked with the chiefs of the 44 South Vietnamese provinces, and mobile advisory teams composed of two officers and three noncommissioned officers, specially trained in infantry weapon and medical aid skills, assisted in the training and deployment of Vietnamese Regional Forces and Popular Forces, whose contribution to local security relieves Vietnamese regular forces for offensive operations.

The so-called *Chieu Hoi* program, under which enemy personnel are encouraged to defect, continued to score successes. Since the program was launched in 1963, over 100,000 of the enemy have rallied to the government of the Republic of Vietnam, some 30,000 during the past year, largely in response to the efforts of psychological operations units.

Elsewhere in Southeast Asia, the 539th Engineer Construction Advisory Detachment operated in Thailand, supporting rural development projects and helping the Royal Thai Army maintain and operate road-building equipment and conduct training. The 97th Civil Affairs Group on Okinawa also deployed mobile training teams to Thailand, and provided a team to South Korea and assistance in Okinawa. The 97th Civil Affairs Group, a component of the Special Action Force, Asia, trains indigenous forces to organize and conduct civic action programs that will strengthen the economic, social, and political conditions in host countries.

In Latin America the 3d Civil Affairs Group, stationed in the Panama Canal Zone, provided veterinary instruction in Bolivia, supply management instruction in Argentina, well-drilling instruction in Paraguay, and surveys of water resources in Panama. The Latin American program has improved co-ordination among governmental agencies in the host countries, leading to concerted planning to attain common goals.

Army psychological operations forces were deployed around the world during fiscal year 1969. One group, with three battalions, was stationed at Fort Bragg, North Carolina, and served as the training, rotational, and augmentation base for deployed units. This group supported the U.S. Army Institute for Military Assistance at the home station.

Another psychological operations group composed of four tactical battalions was deployed in Vietnam to support the Military Assistance Command there. The units carried out air and ground loudspeaker missions; printed and distributed leaflets, safe conduct passes, posters, news sheets, and other materials; made radio and television broadcasts and provided audio-visual services; trained Vietnamese psychological operations units; and supported refugee, public safety, and Vietnamese public information programs.

Another psychological operations group with one battalion and a strategic detachment was located on Okinawa and supplied support detachments in Vietnam, Korea, Taiwan, Thailand, and Japan. Its principal activity was to provide backup printing support to the Military Assistance Command in Vietnam, radio broadcasting and leaflet support to the United Nations Command in Korea, and psychological operations intelligence support to major elements of the Pacific Command. It produced magazines, posters, almanacs, calendars, newspapers, and other psychological materials for distribution to the Korean armed forces and civilian sources in the Republic of Korea, conducted much of the active psychological operations program that involves cold war missions in Korea, and provided radio and visual production support for U.S. psychological operations in the Ryukyu Islands, where a monthly magazine and radio programs are produced that constitute important means of communications for the High Commissioner.

One psychological operations company helped the Royal Thai armed forces develop and execute their PSYOP (psychological operations) program. U.S. Army commanders in Europe and Panama were each supported by one PSYOP battalion.

U.S. Special Forces also supported U.S. Army stability operations during the year and helped develop, organize, train, equip, and direct indigenous forces to conduct unconventional warfare. During the 1969 fiscal year, units continued their missions in Germany, Panama, Okinawa, Thailand, Vietnam, and the United States. The majority of the 10th Special Forces Group was redeployed from Germany to Fort Devens, Massachusetts, in September 1968, and the augmentation detachment assigned to the 46th Special Forces Company in Thailand to assist in training the Thai division staging for Vietnam completed its mission.

The 5th Special Forces Group continued to manage the Civilian Irregular Defense Group program in Vietnam, under which indigenous irregulars have been trained to deny the enemy the use of infiltration routes along the Laotian and Cambodian borders. The group also conducted a wide range of stability operations, such as rural construction, civic action, tactical training, and psychological operations. Other units operated in Thailand, on Okinawa, in Panama, and at the training base at Fort Bragg, North Carolina, assisting host nations and maintaining their special capabilities in this field.

Strategic Mobility

Strategic mobility—the capability to deploy and sustain operational forces anywhere in the world to support national objectives—is one of the elements of national defense that contributes to deterrence. It is based on force deployability, prepositioned materiel, airlift, and sealift. The deployability of Strategic Reserve divisions improved substantially during the year, although there was an increase in deployability times at year-end.

The readiness of Strategic Reserve divisions improved substantially during the year just completed, as noted above, while the concept of prepositioning materiel was demonstrated effectively by the Reforger exercise in Europe, where additional facilities for controlled humidity storage were under construction. Although the level of prepositioning has been depressed by war requirements, plans have been made to reconstitute stocks as resources become available.

The Army continues to support a strategic airlift force of six squadrons of C–5A aircraft, together with an appropriate mix of C–141 and Civil Reserve Air Fleet aircraft, and supports an improvement in the American flagship posture, and the procurement of fast deployment logistics ships, whose authorization and funding were deferred in the 1969 budget.

Communications-Electronics

Over the past several years it became increasingly apparent that the responsiveness of the worldwide communications system could be seriously jeopardized in a time of crisis unless communications discipline was markedly improved. Among the problems were a large volume of high precedence messages, an excessive number of personnel authorized to release messages, excessively long messages, and the use of electrical transmission means for routine purposes. To improve communications discipline, a message monitoring system was established Army-wide in fiscal year 1969, supported by a reporting requirement and departmental analysis. The results were so favorable that the program will be continued and expanded in 1970.

Consolidation, compatibility, and standardization continue to be important considerations in the communications field, and there were a number of developments along these lines in the past year. In July 1968, for example, the Office of the Secretary of Defense directed that communications centers and message centers be consolidated into telecommunications centers serving all geographically collocated subscribers. This will be accomplished gradually without disrupting communications operations. As a part of the action, it was directed that communications centers and message centers be consolidated under a single manager—the communications-electronics officer. Under other programs, significant progress was made regarding the compatibility and standardization of communications systems and equipment.

With an ever-increasing number of communication electronic devices competing for nearly the same frequencies in the electromagnetic spectrum, the Army in 1964 undertook to develop automated procedures that would assist field commanders to make frequency assignments rapidly. Separate studies of radio teletype, tactical voice radio, and radio relay communications networks have produced frequency assignment procedures that will operate on automatic data processing equipment. Field tests in the U.S. Army, Europe, and Seventh Army environment have demonstrated that the procedures can be applied by tactical communications personnel and that effective frequency assignments can be made in less time under the new method. The procedures will be incorporated in training courses and integrated in Army tactical units throughout the world.

To take advantage of technological advances in the audio-visual field and make them available in Army combat training, information display, safety, and other areas of application, an Army-wide study on audio-visual activities was made during the year. Organization and management programs were reviewed and actions will follow on numerous recommendations.

Civil Defense

The strategic objective of our general nuclear war forces is to deter a deliberate nuclear attack upon the United States. If deterrence fails and such a war should occur, the problem and the challenge of civil defense, a vital part of the national defense system, is to limit damage to our people, resources, and institutions. Repeated damage-limiting studies clearly demonstrate the necessity of a nationwide fallout shelter program.

Since 1961, the Office of Civil Defense has concentrated on the development of the nationwide fallout shelter system. By the end of fiscal year 1969, approximately 192.5 million fallout shelter spaces, with a protection factor (Pf) of 40 or better, had been located through various surveys. Pf expresses the relation between the amounts of radiation that would be received by an unprotected person and a person inside the shelter. An unprotected person would receive 40 times more radiation than the person inside a shelter with a Pf of 40.

The National Fallout Shelter Survey, conducted for the Office of Civil Defense by the U.S. Army Corps of Engineers and the U.S. Navy Facilities Engineering Command, identifies dual-use space (that which has a peacetime day-to-day use) in existing structures. At the close of the year, this survey had located 195,751 facilities with public fallout-protected space for 188.2 million people. About 119.7 million of these spaces were licensed, 105.1 million marked with shelter signs, and 58.5 million stocked with federal supplies sufficient to sustain occupants for 14 days or, if shelter areas were filled to their rated capacities, 96.6 million occupants for 8 days.

Civil defense works on a day-to-day basis with all 50 state governments and with the governments of thousands of local jurisdictions, and it receives support from over 300 national organizations and thousands of community leaders and individuals.

The Office of Civil Defense, with the assistance of universities, institutes, and professional societies, has qualified more than 18,000 architects and engineers in the technology of fallout shelter design and analysis. These architects and engineers know how to design buildings to increase inherent fallout protection at little or no additional cost. The Office of Civil Defense also offers professional advisory services to architects and their clients. Many of the fallout shelter spaces added to the nation's expanding shelter inventory are attributable to public and private developers, industrial firms, and others, who use these professional advisory services and apply the principles of radiation shielding in their construction programs.

During the year, the Direct Mail Shelter Development System (DMSDS) was expanded and is now functioning in 38 states. It is essentially a systematic procedure for contacting and encouraging architects and owners of proposed buildings to use design techniques that provide fallout protection. By the end of fiscal year 1969, the DMSDS had processed 11,000 projects in 38 states. Architects for 4,100 projects responded, 37 percent of the project mailing. Approximately 36 percent of those responding requested technical assistance. Results to date indicate that 400 building projects valued at a total of more than $512 million would yield 248 thousand shelter spaces with architect acceptance of DMSDS advice. The cost to the building owner would be approximately $7.15 per shelter space, representing about 0.3 percent of the total valuation of the building projects. Based on these results, arrangements have been made to expand the DMSDS program to 43 states at the beginning of fiscal year 1970.

In addition, the Home Fallout Protection Survey had been completed in 28 states. This survey was conducted by interview or mail questionnaire. In the completed areas 87 percent of the contacted householders responded to the survey. Completed surveys revealed that homes with basements provide significant fallout protection for 30 million people. Nearly all of those not having the national standard of 40 Pf could be readily upgraded to that standard.

Another important aspect of the shelter program, community shelter planning (CSP), continued to expand during the fiscal year. CSP is designed to develop procedures in local communities for making efficient use of the best available protection against radioactive fallout and to provide information to the public on where to go and what to do in the event of an attack. CSP also identifies in geographic detail the unfilled requirements for fallout shelter. At the end of the fiscal year, CSP projects completed or in progress covered 1,409 counties with a total population of 88 million people.

To help assure the effective use of shelters and the conduct of recovery operations, the development of the following civil defense emergency operations systems was continued: (1) a nationwide warning system to alert people to impending attack and to have them take shelter; (2) communications systems to keep people informed and to direct emergency operations; (3) nationwide radiological monitoring and reporting systems to collect, evaluate, and disseminate information on fallout; and (4) a damage assessment system to provide guidance for preattack planning and postattack operations.

Emergency operating centers (EOC's) are needed at the seat of government at all levels for effective executive direction and control in any widespread emergency. These EOC's are fallout-protected centers, planned, staffed, equipped, and provided with communications and warning capability for key officials to use in directing emergency operations. There are 3,099 state and local EOC's established or in the process of being established.

Actions are being taken to tie these EOC's to the Emergency Broadcast System (EBS). This is a system managed by the Federal Communications Commission in co-operation with the commercial broadcast industry to provide the public promptly with official information in an attack emergency. As part of this system, OCD is providing a broadcast station protection program for fallout protection, emergency power where needed, and radio program links connecting EOC's to key EBS stations. This will make it possible for key stations to stay on the air in a fallout environment. By the end of the fiscal year, 617 radio stations were included in this program.

All states and more than 4,400 local governments participating in the civil defense program submitted annual program papers, one of the requirements for eligibility to receive federal civil defense assistance. Federal assistance includes technical guidance, training and education, and surplus property donations, as well as financial assistance.

Other civil defense supporting activities included research to develop an improved technical basis for program direction and guidance; warehousing and control of emergency supplies; prepositioning of emergency public information to inform the public of actions to take in an emergency; community service activities to gain the participation of industry, national organizations, professional associations, institutions, and agencies; and liaison with other elements of the federal government and with civil defense authorities of friendly countries.

The Army has primary service responsibility for military support of civil defense functions within the continental United States, and all services recognize the need for a strong civil defense program. The services represent a major source of assistance to civil defense because of their organization, specialized equipment, disciplined manpower, and long experience in dealing with emergencies.

State adjutants general, when federalized as state area commanders, exercise operational employment over military units made available for postattack military support of civil defense missions within each state. The Commanding General, U.S. Continental Army Command, and the continental U.S. (CONUS) Army commanders exercise preattack military support of civil defense planning guidance over the CONUS-based adjutants general while in a state status. In Alaska, Hawaii, and Puerto Rico, similar preattack and postattack arrangements are the responsibility of the appropriate unified command.

The Army, with DOD approval, is authorized to establish reinforcement training units (RTU's) with members drawn from the Individual Ready Reserve. Members earn retirement point credit for participation in civil defense training. RTU's are authorized to perform preattack planning and training in either civil defense or military support of civil defense. RTU's are not intended to be postattack operational units.

III. Force Development

The Army's force development mission encompasses the organization, training, and mobilization of ground forces. To carry it out the Army develops plans, concepts, and doctrine and determines therefrom how forces will be structured, manned, and equipped. In fiscal year 1969 this responsibility was shaped by the immediate influences of the war in Vietnam and the longer range task of matching resources with estimated requirements progressively into the future.

Plans and Programs

The Army Force Development Plan is the principal document that guides the current integration of resources for the Army. It develops in detail the approved force structure, analyzes it for weaknesses, and proposes corrective action. Published annually, it knits together the complex structure, organization, equipment, concepts, doctrine, personnel, and funding needs for the approved land force. The fiscal year 1969 plan was developed from guidance on strategy, objectives, and forces set out in directives from higher authority.

The instrument that sets the guidelines into the future is a 20-year plan that advances annually. The Army Force Development Plan (AFDP) 1970–89 was developed against a background of strategic concepts, estimates, and assumptions, and in the light of Army missions and undertakings. Approved in May 1969, it focused on the 1972 baseline force—distribution of active and reserve component forces; strength and composition of division forces; requirements for special mission forces; and the adequacy of personnel, materiel, and modernization programs. Certain disparities were revealed: distribution of division initial and sustaining support increments between the active Army and reserves does not match programed strategic lift resources; structural changes have created imbalances in the 48,000-man division force package; there are imbalances between special mission and general support forces; priorities must be set to correct manpower deficiencies; resources must be adjusted to correct equipment deficiencies; civilian to military manpower ratios must be adjusted; and materiel modernization plans must match force development plans. Over-all, the AFDP 1970–89 was more responsive to Army- and Defense-wide planning systems than in previous years, and a number of proposals and recommendations were approved by the Office of the Secretary of Defense.

In fiscal year 1968 a Modular Force Planning System was developed to calculate support unit requirements for a theater of operations. Identified as the "battalion slice," the computerized model was developed on the philosophy that all support units in a theater are there to provide supplies, maintenance, and services to combat units whose mission is to engage the enemy. The system produces a fully structured and theater-oriented troop list by table of organization and equipment and calculates total personnel strength, tonnages, cubages, and costs of the force. The model was tested in October 1968 and accepted in February 1969 for Army Staff use.

The use of data from the force accounting system to identify current, programed, and planned personnel authorizations, materiel requirements, and force computations increased greatly during fiscal year 1969. Refinement of the system, purification of its data, relationship with other automated systems, and improved procedures have made it possible to provide the Army Staff with accurate data through which to manage Army resources.

Automation was also applied in another area of force planning during the year. Project Forewon is a research effort to design an automated force planning system for determining Army general purpose land force requirements and capabilities. The objective is to develop a system of computerized models through which it would be possible to examine a wide range of force planning problems more thoroughly and rapidly than is possible with existing techniques and procedures. A second objective is to carry forward basic research in parallel with system design to advance the state of the art. The major models that comprise the system address such functional areas as combat forces, support forces, force costs, and strategic mobility resources. Each model was designed to operate independently. During fiscal 1969, model design, programing, and validation were completed. An extensive test was begun in June and will be completed in September 1969. It is anticipated that the system will become fully operational in fiscal year 1970, to support the Army Planning System.

Training and Schooling

The expansion of the Army and the buildup in Southeast Asia both reached a crest early in fiscal year 1969, and the remainder of the year saw appropriate adjustments in the training picture. The training base was reduced in August 1968 from 590 to 560 basic combat training companies, and as the year progressed, infantry advanced individual training companies were cut from 130 to 110. During fiscal year 1968, 533,100 active Army and 32,510 Reserve Enlistment Program trainees entered the training base. In fiscal year 1969 the totals were 455,800 and 67,472 respectively.

The plan to equip all basic combat training units with the M–16 rifle, a conversion scheduled for completion in fiscal year 1969, had to be modified as a result of diversions to the high priority modernization program for South Vietnamese troops. Thus only units at Fort Gordon, Georgia, and Fort Jackson, South Carolina, were equipped with the new rifle. Conversion is now scheduled to be completed in February 1970.

Since the inception of Project 100,000, under which youths with correctable educational deficiencies or minor physical defects are accepted and given remedial attention, over 146,000 men have been accepted by the Army. About 12 percent of all accessions without prior service fall into this category; 36 percent have a score below fifth grade reading level; 84.3 percent have been given remedial reading to assist them in basic and advanced training. (The remedial reading program was modified in September 1968, when the training was opened to all eligibles and was scheduled to be conducted prior to basic combat training. Those who require remedial training and complete it enter the second week of basic combat training.) Otherwise, these men are trained at the regular centers and schools and in approximately 170 occupational specialties, of which about 150 are related to civilian-type skills and trades. At present about 42 percent are assigned to combat skills and 58 percent in support skills. Over 90 percent of Project 100,000 men are performing adequately in their jobs.

The Army school system continued to meet worldwide requirements for trained personnel. Priority was given to training that supported Southeast Asia requirements. In fiscal year 1969, 413,000 personnel entered Army schools.

The skill development base program has had considerable impact on Army training concepts, manpower management, and the ability of the Army to fill its requirements in grades E–5 and E–6. The objective of the program is to train individuals so that they may perform satisfactorily in their initial duty assignment. This training is undertaken immediately following basic combat and advanced individual training and is normally of 21 to 24 weeks' duration. During fiscal year 1969 approximately 11,600 enlisted men were graduated from 42 courses of instruction and promoted to either E–5 or E–6 under this program. Reports from commanders in Vietnam indicate that these men are doing well in combat.

The Army's civil schooling program, which provides military personnel with advanced education to fill validated requirements for senior staff, technical, and school positions, was expanded during the past year. An average of 990 students were enrolled in the program and 649 completed their studies during 1969 and received degrees. An additional 462 personnel attended short specialized courses at civilian institutions.

As a result of an increased aviation training output of 610 pilots per month beginning in July 1968, the Army now trains more aviators than all of the other services combined. In addition to the 7,561 active Army pilots trained in fiscal year 1969, the Army also trained 150 U.S. Marine Corps pilots and 180 foreign military students.

The Reserve Officers' Training Corps (ROTC) program continues to be a viable one, this year producing over 16,000 officers, the largest number from any source for any service. It also continues to be the least expensive commissioning program in the Army. During the year, new policies and curricula were developed for Senior ROTC that would tailor the program to meet the combined needs of the Army, the institution, and the student. In fiscal year 1969 the program flourished. However, there was a marked increase in the number of anti-ROTC incidents, in addition to certain faculty and student attacks on curriculum content, academic credit, professorial rank, and the availability and use of facilities.

The Officer Candidate School (OCS) program provided the Army with 8,900 commissioned officers during the year. The course for male officers, 23 weeks in length, is conducted at Fort Benning, Georgia, Fort Sill, Oklahoma, and Fort Belvoir, Virginia. The Women's Army Corps OCS is 18 weeks in length and is conducted at Fort McClellan, Alabama. Fiscal year 1970 production is presently programed at a level of 9,300 officers for all courses.

A U.S. Army War College nonresident course was initiated in fiscal year 1969. Its purpose is to prepare senior active Army and reserve component officers for command and key staff responsibilities at major military and departmental headquarters. The nonresident course was conceived to supply qualitative augmentation to the production of the regular course at the Army War College at Carlisle Barracks, Pennsylvania. The new course provides added depth to the active Army educational base and fills a void in military education for officers of the Army reserve components. About 200 qualified officers are selected for participation annually, half from the active Army and half from among Ready Reservists not on active duty.

The correspondence study program closely parallels the resident course at the Army War College. Both have the same curricular theme— the development of a national strategy and a supporting program. The nonresident course extends over a 2-year period. The studies in the primary areas of strategic appraisal, strategy, and military planning require from three to seven hours per week of the student's off-duty time. A 2-week resident phase at Carlisle Barracks is scheduled in the summer at mid-course. The first class will graduate in the summer of 1970.

Although the primary purpose of all Army training and schooling is to prepare personnel to further the Army's role in national defense, attention is given to their eventual return to civilian life and their future roles as citizens. Project Transition is a program designed to make available to military personnel in-service training and educational opportunities that will increase their chances for employment in civilian life. It is primarily concerned with personnel who were poorly educated or had no marketable civilian skill when brought into the Army and were unable to improve their civilian job potential before separation. Assistance is afforded in vocational skill training, counseling, and educational upgrading; attention is centered on helping personnel attain high-school-level background. Substantial assistance is being received from both the public and private sectors. Length of training courses ranges from two to six weeks with a wide variety of subjects offered. Fifty-five CONUS Army installations are currently participating in the program.

Doctrine and Systems

The size, complexity, and cost of military systems today requires that they be kept under constant surveillance and review. During fiscal year 1969 there were reviews of a number of systems and programs. In the functional area, for example, the first infantry battalion system review was held at Fort Benning, Georgia, to consider the infantry battalion as a combat system, its organization, and its training requirements.

The combat vehicle program was reviewed twice in the fiscal year, with special attention being focused on the M–551 Sheridan, the M–60A1E2 tank, and the main battle tank 1970. The Army aviation program was appraised, an artillery program review was held to formulate development and procurement up through the 1980's, and the air defense program was reviewed to evaluate the Army's worldwide situation in this regard.

An Army small arms program was established in January 1968 to provide direction and guidance over small arms development. Two major conferences were held on this subject during the fiscal year, and in November 1968 the U.S. Army Small Arms Systems Agency began limited operations leading to its eventual assumption of management responsibility for most small arms systems.

During the year a new stock for the M–16A1 rifle was developed and tested; it provides a compartment for the rifleman's cleaning equipment. The XM–203 40-mm. grenade launcher attachment for this rifle was also completed and was tested in Vietnam. Meanwhile, conversion to this new rifle continued. The older M–1 and M–14 rifles are being replaced as the M–16A1 becomes available and the South Vietnamese modernization program is completed.

The development of modern tools of war, whether rifles or tanks, helicopters or missiles, is highly expensive, increasingly technical, unusually complex, and always advancing. Various elements and characteristics—ammunition, propulsion, fuel, optics, communications, guidance, protection, mobility, weight, size—are constantly evolving and changing as technology advances. In major combat vehicles, for example, numerous elements must be blended in appropriate combinations, taking full advantage of, and indeed advancing, the state of the art. Alternatives in any and all component parts of any system must be investigated. The combination that is selected may be the only feasible solution and will usually represent a compromise between competing characteristics. Some lines of developmental investigation will prove fruitless; some development will fall short of expectations; some prototypes will fail to make the grade; some production models will contain bugs. Yet the most unprofitable lines of inquiry and the most unsuccessful test models are not failures; all contribute to the sum of knowledge, help point the way to success, play a part in the process through which the Army insures that materiel placed in the hands of troops will be the best that brains, technology, energy, money, facilities, and time will allow.

Within this context, there were problems and progress in Army combat weapons systems during fiscal year 1969. Several systems received national attention as a result of press coverage, citizen opposition, congressional consideration, and Army action, among them the Sentinel-Safeguard, the Cheyenne helicopter, the main battle tank 1970, and the Sheridan armored assault vehicle.

The Cheyenne (AH–56A) was conceived as an integrated aerial weapons system, a high-speed and heavily armed helicopter to escort airmobile forces and provide direct fire support. Following award of the production contract, technical difficulties arose in the prototype aircraft. On May 19, 1969, when it appeared that production schedules would not be met with aircraft that would meet performance specifications, the production contract was terminated by the Army for default. As the year closed, the Cheyenne program was being evaluated to determine a course of action that would make maximum use of the work to date.

Broad public and congressional attention also centered on the M–551 armored reconnaissance assault vehicle. Named the Sheridan, this is a lightly armored, highly mobile, heavy gun system designed for airborne assault use. During fiscal year 1969 the Sheridan was deployed to Vietnam, Korea, and Europe for combat evaluation and training purposes. The battlefield assessment was completed in May 1969 and the Sheridan was found to be an effective mobile weapon readily responsive to the roles and missions of armored cavalry units. The vehicle performed well in the battlefield test, although problems were identified that will require correction.

Joint development on the main battle tank (MBT) by the United States and the Federal Republic of Germany continued during the year, with the range of problems to be expected when an entirely new tank is being created from the ground up. As in all hardware development, this program has been subjected to inflationary pressures. The MBT is scheduled for production in the mid-1970's and will incorporate the latest advances in engines, transmissions, fire control, suspension, automatic loading, armor protection, and human engineering. It will be manufactured in both countries, using common components and logistical support.

Development continued on a new infantry antitank-assault weapon family. As a result of testing in Vietnam, the M–72 light antitank-assault weapon (LAW) was refined, an improved warhead was produced for use in Vietnam, and new development objectives were set for a future model that would be fielded after 1975. Engineering development continued on the DRAGON medium antitank-assault weapon, and while no serious technical difficulties were encountered, management problems led to a complete program review. And finally, engineering and service testing (less environmental tests) was completed on the heavy version weapon in the family, the TOW. Production had begun as the year closed, with the first missile to be delivered in August 1969 and the first unit to be equipped in September 1970.

The performance of the PERSHING missile system and its readiness to serve in a quick reaction role improved during the 1969 fiscal year. Development and testing of ground support equipment continued on schedule. Service test of the PERSHING IA missile system was completed in August 1968 and the initial production test was completed in March 1969. Deployment in the continental U.S. training base began in April 1969.

In the field of surface-to-surface missiles, the LANCE moved along in the research and development phase while the system launching and transporting equipment reached the technical maturity levels required for production. This missile will replace the LITTLE JOHN, HONEST JOHN, and SERGEANT systems.

Army air defense forces were reduced during the year by 21 active Army and 4 Army National Guard NIKE-HERCULES firing batteries in 10 defense areas throughout the continental United States. The total defenses at St. Louis, Kansas City, and Dallas–Fort Worth were eliminated, while batteries were inactivated in the defenses of New England, New York–Philadelphia, Washington–Baltimore, Pittsburgh, Detroit, Chicago-Milwaukee, and Los Angeles.

As the HERCULES system will be in the Army tactical inventory well beyond the life cycle projected for it when it was deployed in 1958, it will be modified to extend its usefulness to a later phaseout. The surface-to-air missile capability (SAMCAP) program was funded in the fiscal year 1969 budget. The program will increase the missile maneuverability and improve the electronic countermeasures capability of the HERCULES system.

The Army has been updating the basic HAWK missile system to make it more reliable, more lethal, and more useful tactically. The improved version will have increased range and altitude. To this end, engineering and flight test programs were completed during the year. The self-propelled version of the HAWK, with capabilities of the basic system, also moved along; training was begun in U.S. Army, Europe, and orders were issued directing the reorganization of the HAWK battalions in that command.

The SAM–D surface-to-air missile system will eventually replace the NIKE-HERCULES and HAWK. Advanced development continued during fiscal year 1969, with favorable indications as to technical progress. Procurement proceeded on the CHAPARRAL-Vulcan system, designed to defend the field Army against low altitude attacks.

In the Army aviation area, initial delivery was made on a 5-year procurement contract for 2,200 OH–58A Kiowa light observation helicopters, a single-engine craft designed to serve in armed reconnaissance, visual observation, target acquisition, and command and control.

Sentinel-Safeguard

In September 1967, the Army was instructed to proceed with the deployment of a ballistic missile defense system, using the NIKE-X program as a platform. Its primary purpose was to provide area protection to U.S. population centers against a possible Chinese missile attack in the 1970's, and additionally to offer an option to defend this country's land-based deterrent forces against a larger Soviet threat, should that occur. The Sentinel ballistic missile defense system, as it came to be known, consisted of five basic components: two types of radars (perimeter acquisition radar and missile site radar); two missiles (long-range SPARTAN and shorter range SPRINT); and a data processing (computer) system. As a "thin" (limited) deployment, Sentinel was to be installed originally at 17 geographical locations, among which were the metropolitan areas of Boston, Chicago, Detroit, Seattle, San Francisco, and Los Angeles. The first site, that at Boston, was to be ready by October 1972, the last in October 1974.

During late calendar year 1967 and early 1968, surveys were carried out on several potential sites to determine the best location for planned facilities. At the same time, certain preliminary engineering was also accomplished. Between July and December 1968, the Army notified

Congress that it was proceeding to acquire land for sites in the vicinity of Boston, Chicago, and Seattle.

However, as a result of opposition to the program and certain changes in the threat, a newly elected administration began a reassessment of the Sentinel system as a part of an over-all strategic posture review. Concurrently, the Secretary of Defense in February 1969 issued a stop order on all land acquisition and site construction activities pending the outcome of the review. Meanwhile, studies were initiated to develop alternative sites away from cities, while research and development was to continue without interruption. In the reformulation of the deployment, basic considerations included a shift in emphasis from the defense of cities to the defense of deterrent forces; expansion of area defense to include the entire continental United States; and the desirability of incorporating any improvements to interceptors and radars, attained through further research and development, in proportion to the developing threat.

On March 14, 1969, the President, after careful and detailed examination of the program, announced his decision for a Sentinel system modified from that evolved by the previous administration. Under a new and measured deployment, it was conceived to fulfill three basic objectives: (1) safeguard U.S. retaliatory forces against advances made by the Soviet Union; (2) safeguard against any attack which Communist China could mount over the next decade; and (3) safeguard against any irrational or accidental attack of a lesser magnitude from any source. The President emphasized the "safeguard" or defensive character of such deployment, and out of the new concept came a new designation— Safeguard system—which took effect on March 25, 1969. An annual review and assessment of the program would gauge the need for its continuation or expansion, depending upon periodic analysis of the developing threat, technical system advances, and progress in reaching a strategic arms limitation agreement.

The presidential decision attempted in a sense to occupy the middle ground, holding the system's deployment to modest proportions while permitting a cautious flexibility for the future. The reaction in Congress and among members of the scientific community was mixed, forecasting an intensification of opposing views as to the direction the program should follow.

Within the framework of the new objectives, Phase I of the limited deployment is to be at two MINUTEMAN sites only, those at Grand Forks Air Force Base in North Dakota, and Malmstrom Air Force Base in Montana. The other geographical areas, subject to future congressional consideration, were broadly identified as upper Northwest, central and southern California, southern New England, Wyoming, Missouri,

Florida-Georgia, central Texas, Washington, D.C., and Michigan-Ohio. Appropriate studies were undertaken to validate the tentative system configuration schedules and improve cost estimates wherever possible. In the light of these considerations, a comprehensive system design review was initiated to analyze the effectiveness of the new Safeguard system. The results were forwarded to the Secretary of the Army at the end of May 1969 with a recommendation for approval by the Secretary of Defense.

Throughout fiscal year 1969, considerable progress was made in developing the components of the system. The configuration of the perimeter acquisition radar (PAR) was defined, equipment layout was developed, performance and design specifications were drafted, and a test model was well under way. Construction, started in early 1968 on a prototype missile site radar (MSR), was completed at the Kwajalein Island test area, and the radar installation's data processing and programing activities became partially operational. Static tests were held on the SPRINT missile's ground support equipment and launch procedures, and SPARTAN components were improved for tactical use.

Some $861.4 million of Sentinel funds were made available to Safeguard and applied mostly to research and development, engineering, and production. Another $891.5 million was estimated for fiscal year 1970 funding, while the total Department of Defense investment for the first phase of the program—procurement of components and construction of the Montana and North Dakota sites—was estimated at $2.1 billion. Parallel to the reappraisal that continued throughout the fiscal year, a host of congressional inquiries came to the fore, those in the last quarter especially probing matters of budget allocation. The manpower baseline established by Safeguard encompassed requirements considered essential for limited deployment pending further assessment at the end of 1969.

The ABM program moved back into Congress for approval in its modified form at a time when cost overruns and inflationary pressures were in the national consciousness; when weapons requirements were being balanced against social needs; when estimates of the external threat were being questioned; when arms limitation talks were in the offing; and when there was something less than unanimity in the scientific community over the technical feasibility of the ballistic missile defense system. Controversy centered on all of these issues and the debate in Congress continued heatedly throughout the closing quarter of the year. As fiscal year 1969 came to an end, it appeared that the vote in the United States Senate on delpoyment of the Safeguard would come before the summer recess.

IV. Personnel

The Army's personnel mission embodies the recruitment, training and schooling, assignment and utilization, compensation, discipline, health and welfare, spiritual sustenance, safety, and morale of military and civilian manpower. In fiscal year 1969 this mission was shaped by the size of the Army, its worldwide deployment, the war in Vietnam, and, above all, the requirement to maintain personnel levels in the theater of operations under the stringencies of the short tour turnover.

Military Personnel*

For the first time in several years, the Army's strength decreased in fiscal year 1969, from 1,570,343 to 1,512,169, a reflection of the leveling off of the war, the inactivation of the 6th Infantry Division, and a lower trainee population. There were 2,532 cadets, 172,590 officers, and 1,337,047 enlisted personnel. With 37,536 officer accessions during the year, the year-end officer strength was the highest since World War II. A total of 254,279 men were inducted into the Army and 200,897 men and women were acquired by first enlistment—a decrease of 79,943 in inductions and an increase of 2,037 in enlistments over the previous year.

Army strength continued to rise in Vietnam—from 355,000 to 361,000—but at a slower pace than during 1968. The 6,000 augmentation represented a 1.7 percent rise as compared with a 15 percent increase in fiscal year 1968.

Battle casualties were high during the fiscal year period. The Army had 7,653 killed and 53,034 wounded through hostile action; 30,652 of the wounded were returned to duty without hospital care. Total Army casualties over the course of the war from January 1961 through June 1969 numbered 23,324 killed and 149,265 wounded, and over half of the wounded were returned to duty without requiring hospital care.

Since July 1965 the Army has sustained a rate of 21.6 deaths per 1,000 troop strength per year as compared with a World War II battle death rate for active theaters of 37.4 per 1,000 troop strength per year. The rate in the European Theater of Operations alone for the year ending in May 1945 was 51.9 per 1,000 troop strength.

While reporting requirements for deaths have changed very little since 1941, there has been a marked change in casualty reporting of the

*Strength figures include reimbursables.

wounded since the end of the Korean War. Earlier casualty reports were submitted on wounded personnel who were admitted to hospital and other medical treatment facilities. Reports on Army casualties in Vietnam include personnel who receive minor injuries due to hostile action and are treated on an outpatient or duty status without admission, as well as those who are excused from duty for treatment. Casualty reports compiled in Vietnam reveal that 95.2 Army personnel were wounded per 1,000 troop strength per year. In the Korean War the nonfatal, wounded in action rate was 121.1 per 1,000 troop strength per year; in World War II the figure was 90.1 in all active theaters and 152.0 in the European Theater of Operations during the 12 months ending in May 1945.

As of June 30, 1968, 185 Army personnel were missing in action in Vietnam and 27 were known to be prisoners of the enemy. As of June 30, 1969, Army casualties in these categories totaled 206 missing and 46 captured.

To insure that individual achievement, whether in or out of action, is identified and recognized in a timely manner, award procedures have been decentralized to some degree in Vietnam over the past two years. Separate brigade commanders were authorized to award the Bronze Star, while commanders at the level of major general were authorized to award the Silver Star. Final approval for the award of the Distinguished Service Medal remains with the Army Chief of Staff, while the President is the final approving authority for the Medal of Honor. The magnitude of recognition is evident in the fact that in calendar year 1968 a total of 427,823 decorations in all categories from the Purple Heart to the Medal of Honor were awarded, while another 318,345 were awarded in the first six months of 1969.

Sustaining U.S. Army deployments in Vietnam, Thailand, and Korea has been one of the major concerns over the period of the Army expansion and the Vietnam buildup. There are numerous facets to such a process. It has been necessary, for example, to meet the short tour (12 months) replacement turnover in Vietnam with the required numbers of individuals in the proper grades and skills, while maintaining the short tour policy in other areas, the long tour objectives (25 months) for the continental United States and certain overseas areas, an equitable assignment pattern for the career soldier subject to repetitive tours, an efficient training base, and a readiness posture against other contingencies. Of the approximate one-and-a-half-million men and women in the Army, some 700,000 are serving overseas at any one time. Of the more than 800,000 serving in the United States, over 197,000 are trainees not ready for assignment. This suggests the difficulty of maintaining the rapid turnover and providing qualified replacements.

There are almost a thousand different categories of military skill, and these are not distributed equally between long and short tour areas. For example, there are $10\frac{1}{3}$ division forces in short tour areas and $9\frac{1}{3}$ in long tour areas. The disparity is even more marked where certain types of support units are concerned; a high percentage of individuals possessing certain skills are needed in short tour areas. A large proportion of the Army's enlisted requirements are in skills which are not self-sustaining because the requirements for them in long tour areas are inadequate to provide a rotation base for short tour areas.

The effect of an inadequate rotation base has been to create a high level of personnel movement and turbulence throughout the sustaining base units of the Army. This has led to reduced readiness in the forces outside Vietnam and compromised to some degree the 25-month base tour objective. It has meant that 2,162 personnel were returned involuntarily to short tour areas in fiscal year 1968, and 8,952 in fiscal year 1969, before completing their base tours.

Another problem associated with the Vietnam buildup has been a decrease in experience levels throughout the Army. The 56 percent increase in Army strength since 1965 has been attained through increased accessions of untrained draftees and enlistees who stay in the Army for only two or three years. Currently, about half of the Army's commissioned officers and two-thirds of its enlisted men have less than two years of service. In spite of the expansion, there are 100,000 fewer enlisted careerists today than there were before the buildup. Career soldiers—individuals with more than three years of service—numbered nearly 400,000 in 1964; by 1969, with over half-a-million more men in the Army, the career force has been reduced by 25 percent to less than 300,000. The result is a chronic shortage of officers and enlisted men in the middle grades.

Several steps have been taken to sustain short tour deployments and relieve constraints in the middle grades. Short tour personnel returning to the United States with less than 150 days of service remaining have been discharged, obviating their assignment to units for such brief periods that they contribute little to unit readiness and much to personnel turbulence. Also, personnel have been encouraged to extend their tour of duty voluntarily in the combat area, with a 30-day leave as an incentive to a 6-month extension; short term extensions to create eligibility for separation under the 150-day early release program have also promoted stability. Yet another procedure has been to revise assignment priorities in selected units, permitting them to conduct more progressive training and reach higher levels of readiness while maintaining a stable personnel situation.

Two actions in skill development also furthered the equalization process. Output from the skill development base program was accelerated, rising from about 4,500 in fiscal year 1968 to over 12,000 in 1969 and helping to fill the middle grade leadership gap; and the number of individuals trained in skills critical to Vietnam was increased to meet short tour replacement requirements (for example, 9,100 more riflemen and 2,800 more aviation mechanics were trained than would normally have been the case).

Finally, a word is in order concerning the Reserve contribution in this problem area. The call-up of approximately 20,000 Reservists provided a source of experienced middle-grade leaders. Of the total, about 6,100 of the Reservists were deployed to Southeast Asia with units and 6,000 as individual replacements. The availability of the latter had a stabilizing influence on rotational patterns; many more careerists would have had shortened base tours and been returned to Vietnam involuntarily in fiscal year 1969 had it not been for the Reserve augmentation.

The Army in fiscal year 1969 acquired 37,536 officers and warrant officers.

ACCESSIONS OF OFFICERS BY SOURCE IN FISCAL YEAR 1969

Source	Accessions
Service academies	759
Reserve Officers' Training Corps	14,435
Officer Candidate School	8,807
Voluntary active duty	555
Professional (JAGC, WAC, MSC, CHAP)	1,716
Medical Corps, Dental Corps, Veterinary Corps	3,627
Regular Army appointments (from civil life)	36
Miscellaneous [1]	431
Nurses and medical specialists	1,237
Warrant Officers	5,933
Total [2]	37,536

[1] Includes administrative gains such as recall from retired list and interservice transfers.
[2] Excludes reimbursable personnel.

The total number of warrant officers in the Army increased from 20,185 at the end of fiscal year 1968 to 23,754 at the end of fiscal year 1969. The growth of the warrant officer program is illustrated by the fact that the strength at the beginning of fiscal year 1967 was 11,318. Approximately 47 percent of warrant officer positions are in aviation specialties. About 350 outstanding aviation warrant officers who demonstrated exceptional leadership capabilities and potential were awarded direct commissions during fiscal year 1969.

In another officer acquisition area, the Reserve Officers' Training Corps scholarship program was transferred on July 1, 1968, from departmental headquarters to Headquarters, Continental Army Command. Total scholarships in effect increased from 3,019 in 1968 to 3,907 in

1969; another 2,138 outstanding high school and college students have been selected to receive Army ROTC scholarships for the 1969–70 school year. Eight hundred high school graduates were awarded 4-year scholarships to be used at any of 274 colleges and universities offering the 4-year Army ROTC program in the fall of 1969. Two-year scholarships were awarded to 1,338 outstanding college sophomores who completed two years of ROTC training. The program holds considerable promise for expansion to its statutory limits.

Enlisted procurement and career programs must be constantly reviewed, modified, and updated to fit the needs of the times. The first enlistment option was introduced in 1792. It authorized enlistments for the "Legion of the United States." It appears to have been successful, since in May 1794 the Congress authorized the enlistment of 754 men to serve three years in the Corps of Artillerists and Engineers. Army enlistment options today aim at providing specific training that will encourage qualified men and women to serve in the Regular Army for three or more years. Recently, two new options were established to attract men to the combat arms. A noncommissioned officer candidate course, under which enlistees are assured assignment to a combat arms noncommissioned officer candidate course and promotion to grade E–5 upon graduation, was initiated to fill middle management positions with intelligent and versatile young men. A ranger enlistment option, promising airborne and ranger training and assignment, was developed to provide a new source for volunteers for the recently reactivated 75th Infantry (Merrill's Marauders).

The intensified recruitment program, which concentrates on acquiring men from areas of high unemployment, progressed in fiscal year 1969. Army recruiters were conducting the campaign in 43 major cities and on the Navajo Indian Reservation. Some 12,000 men, about 6 percent of all male enlistments, were recruited from designated poverty areas during the year. The majority were unemployed, were not over 19 years old, had less than an 11th grade education, and scored correspondingly in classification tests.

The Army is establishing an enlisted career management program that is centralized at Department of the Army headquarters. Developed under Project MECCA (Management of Enlisted Careerists, Centrally Administered), the program will be implemented over the course of several years, and eventually will include all soldiers in grade E–5 and above who have completed three years of active service. The concept envisions that each soldier will be developed to the maximum based on his ability and diligence, and individual aptitude will be further cultivated in progressive schooling and assignments of increasing responsibility. The Enlisted Personnel Directorate at departmental headquarters will maintain the career soldier's management file, select his assignments and schooling, and keep him posted on his progress and standing among his contemporaries. Individuals who demonstrate the capacity will be provided with more challenging assignments as well as advanced schooling and opportunities for more rapid advancement. The enlisted management program is aimed at improving the attractiveness of an Army career. In January 1969 one of the important parts of the program was launched—centralized promotion to grades E–8 and E–9. Thus for the first time, promotion to the top two enlisted grades is being made by selection boards on the basis of Army-wide consideration; the best qualified candidates will be elevated, no matter where they are serving around the world.

Increasing numbers of college graduates are entering the Army through induction or enlistment as a result of the termination of graduate deferments. Every effort is being made to benefit both the Army and the individuals by assigning them to activities that make use of their prior training, education, experience, and leadership potential. A survey was made of Army positions and occupational specialties, and three categories of skill were identified against which college graduates could be considered. Priority I embraces skills that can be correlated to academic fields or personal preferences of college graduates, such as officer training, scientific or engineer fields, or language training. Priority II consists of skills that challenge the leadership or technical capabilities of college men, such as combat arms potential, radar technology, or automatic data processing. Priority III comprises skills that are essential but which do not challenge or make use of the background of the average college graduate, for example, driver, cook, or shoe repairman. In fiscal year 1969, 37,246 college graduates were assigned in these general fields of priority: 62.1 percent (23,156) in the priority I area, 37.6 percent (13,944) in priority II, and 0.3 percent in priority III.

The information that is developed on a soldier at the time he enters the service is important both to him and to the Army in connection with the efficient utilization of personnel. To improve the methods by which that initial personnel information is collected, a contract has been awarded to a commercial firm to design, program, and install a new nationwide electronic communications system by means of which personnel data would be transmitted to a central location. This system for consolidation of accessions and trainees (SCAT) will be used to develop personnel data on all enlisted men entering the armed forces and provide information to various Department of Defense users.

In the field of officer utilization, the Military Assistance Officer Program, which incorporated the Civil Affairs Officer Program, has been established to identify and develop personnel for assignment to politico-military positions not only in the Army but throughout the Department of Defense. The program provides a career field for officers who have the skills to conduct required military activities of social, economic, and psychological impact. Training will be conducted at the John F. Kennedy Center for Military Assistance at Fort Bragg, North Carolina. About 1,000 command and staff positions are being considered for designation as key military assistance billets.

The end strength of the Chaplains Branch remained close to the level—1,866—attained at the end of fiscal year 1968. Although an increase of 100 spaces authorized a total strength of 1,925, procurement slowed down considerably toward mid-year, resulting in an end strength of 1,909 for fiscal year 1969. Of these, 1,429 were of Protestant denominations, 438 were Catholic, and 42 were Jewish.

One of the 410 chaplains who served in Vietnam during the fiscal year was killed in action and another died as a result of an aircraft accident. On November 19, 1968, President Lyndon B. Johnson presented to Chaplain (Captain) Angelo J. Liteky the Medal of Honor for heroic action near Phuoc Lac, Vietnam. The first Army chaplain to receive this highest military honor since the Civil War, he was the fourth such recipient in the history of the U.S. Army chaplaincy.

During the third quarter of the fiscal year, workshops for chaplains on the subject "Ministry to the Drug User" were held throughout the Army. The purpose was to prepare chaplains to counsel with and minister to drug users within the military community. Professional assistance from other branches of the Army and from the civilian community was effectively utilized and contributed immeasurably to the success of these workshops.

The professional training of chaplains in their area of pastoral ministry was furthered with the assignment of 15 chaplains to civilian educational institutions for 1-year courses in pastoral counseling.

On May 28, 1968, the Secretary of the Army directed that the Army's Artillery Branch be separated into an Air Defense Artillery Branch and a Field Artillery Branch. The decision was the result of a lengthy study, begun in September 1966, to determine what effect existing officer personnel policies had upon the efficiency of artillery units and the proficiency and career of the artillery officer. The study revealed that there were three categories of artillerymen—one group had served only in field artillery assignments, another had served only in air defense artillery assignments, and the third had served in both. Analysis showed that personnel in the last category had lower achievement levels than the other groups. They also achieved less academically than did those who served only in one field of artillery specialization. The study further revealed that integration of the artillery caused a waste of training time, imposed an unnecessary burden on units with cross-assigned artillerymen, and lowered the traditional professionalism of artillery officers. The separation once again into field artillery and air defense branches permits officers to develop maximum proficiency in their respective arms, improves their competitive chances and standings for promotion and schooling, and furthers combat readiness in units of both branches.

Retention of both officers and enlisted men is always a military personnel problem, and especially so in wartime. Inadequate retention levels since the Korean War have led to the present shortage in the middle grades of officers and enlisted men. Based on past experience, the present retention rate of Regular Army officers is within acceptable limits; for example, the rate for ROTC distinguished military graduates at the 4-year point (one year following the completion of obligated service) has averaged 85 percent, while that for U.S. Military Academy graduates has been 88 percent at the completion of one year following obligated service. Involuntary extension has had some impact on these rates, especially for the 1964 group.

Since the number of Regular officers is limited by statute to 49,500, expanded requirements have made it necessary to retain a large number of non-Regulars as careerists. To sustain an officer corps of 100,000 men, it is estimated that approximately 4,500 other-than-Regular officers must be retained annually as careerists. In recent years an annual average of 2,530 such officers have extended their service voluntarily. Although the ROTC program has been the major source of officers, the expanded officer candidate school program was used to provide the majority of junior officers during the Vietnam buildup. If the fiscal year 1969 retention rate of 27.7 percent (7,502 extensions out of 27,064 eligibles) continues in fiscal year 1970, the current shortage of captains in the Army will be partially alleviated.

Among enlisted personnel it is again in the younger brackets that the most active turnover occurs. Noncommissioned officer re-enlistments have declined since 1965, especially in grades E–5 and E–6. There is a higher proportion of non-Regulars in the middle NCO grades and therefore correspondingly lower re-enlistment rates. In a period of expanded requirements and accelerated promotion opportunity, this will continue to be a matter of concern. The reasons why men leave the service are well identified, and the Army is working along many lines to improve the retention picture.

In the personnel areas that concern separation and retirement, several programs have been going on that are out of ordinary routine. One of these, the early release program, has already been described. Another is the effort to smooth the transition for those departing the service. To insure that a member of the military family receives an appropriate send-off, and to enhance the image of the Army in the minds of those returning to civilian life, separation facilities and procedures were improved and departure ceremonies formalized during the year. In the retirement area, the selective retention program was continued and about 200 of some 1,200 Regular Army officers and warrant officers who applied for retirement were deferred.

During fiscal year 1969 a number of important manpower studies were in progress, primarily concerned with the acquisition and retention of personnel. At the top of the list, a working level investigation was launched to determine whether and how the Army could meet military manpower requirements without relying on the draft. The expansion of the Army and the buildup in Vietnam have been accomplished primarily through conscription, and opposition to the draft has produced increasing speculation over the possibilities of an all-volunteer Army. Any such study must address manpower management and personnel policies as they affect procurement, distribution, sustainment, training, and separation, and must include evaluations of the interaction of four central considerations—quality, quantity, cost, and socioeconomic implications. Ultimately, a package of programs and policies with associated costs will be developed. Meanwhile, a presidential commission composed of distinguished Americans from various walks of life is considering the subject in its national context.

Along more conventional lines, initial staffing on a concept study to guide personnel activities through the middle of the next decade was completed in the fiscal year. Rapid change was identified as the most significant factor in future operations; the principal challenge was anticipated to be that of maintaining personnel stability in a restless social, economic, and political environment.

Even as the Army was dealing with current problems of accession and retention, a study was a progress to determine the kind of officer grade structure that would provide the quality and quantity of leadership the Army needs to carry out its mission up to 1985. Such a structure must hold career appeal and be attainable and sustainable from the present base.

One of the keys to ameliorating the problems in officer career progression, grade balance, promotion patterns, leadership proficiency, and over-all stability rests in junior officer retention. A study of this subject revealed that the factors which most influence a junior officer's decision to leave the service or remain on active duty after completing his obligated service include his duties and his attitude toward them, career management, increased educational opportunities, relationships between personnel of the several components, leadership and morale, financial security, and family considerations. To the extent possible, policy in each of these areas will be adjusted to further officer retention.

Military Justice, Discipline, and Legal Services

There were several pivotal developments in the field of military justice during fiscal year 1969. Of far-reaching significance was the United States Supreme Court's decision, issued on June 2, 1969, in the case of *O'Callahan* versus *Parker*. This ruling holds that courts-martial are without jurisdiction to try soldiers for offenses which are not "service-connected." It specifically decided that the offenses of attempted rape, housebreaking, and assault with intent to rape, committed off post, while on leave, within the jurisdiction of Hawaii, against a civilian victim, and in peacetime, are not "service-connected." The exact limits of the ruling in the *O'Callahan* case and of the jurisdiction of courts-martial will be defined in subsequent cases in both military and civilian courts. The immediate effects of the decision will be the dismissal of certain charges now pending and referral of these charges to civilian courts. Many previously convicted soldiers will now claim that their cases fall within the rule of the *O'Callahan* case, thus generating a great number of collateral attacks on otherwise final cases and a vast number of applications for administrative correction of records and restoration of pay and other benefits.

During the fiscal year the Congress passed the Military Justice Act of 1968, an enactment favored by the Army and the entire Department of Defense. The act, which becomes fully effective on August 1, 1969, makes far-reaching changes in the Uniform Code of Military Justice. It provides the opportunity for accused at special courts-martial to be defended by a qualified lawyer, provides for detailing military judges (formerly called law officers) to special courts-martial, provides an option for trial by military judge alone at all general courts-martial and at those special courts-martial to which a military judge has been detailed, and makes other procedural changes.

In fiscal year 1969, 76,320 persons were tried by court-martial, a rate of 49.92 per 1,000 military strength, as compared with 57,685 in 1968, a rate of 38.14 per 1,000. By types of court-martial, the fiscal year statistics show that 2,482 were tried by general court-martial (1.62 per 1,000) compared with 2,375 in fiscal year 1968 (1.57 per 1,000); 59,597 were tried by special court-martial (38.98 per 1,000) as compared with 43,769 in fiscal year 1968 (28.9 per 1,000); and 14,241 received summary courts-martial (9.32 per 1,000) as compared with 11,541 in fiscal year 1968 (7.63 per 1,000). Under Article 86 of the Uniform Code of Military Justice, 1,158 convictions were handed down for absent-without-leave (AWOL) offenses in fiscal year 1969 as compared with 1,100 in 1968. There were 140 desertion convictions by general court-martial under Article 85 of the code in fiscal year 1969 as compared with 139 the previous year. And 301,095 were punished for lesser offenses under Article 15 of the code (196.9 per 1,000) as compared with 263,612 in fiscal year 1968 (174.3 per 1,000).

Although AWOL and desertion rates per 1,000 enlisted strength increased in fiscal year 1969, they are generally in line with those for 1952 at the peak of the Korean War and those for 1960 in a period of lower Army strength. The increase in the number of military prisoners in confinement challenged the Army's correctional effort.

The U.S. Army's Correctional Training Facility began operation at Fort Riley, Kansas, on July 1, 1968, like the U.S. Disciplinary Barracks, under the command jurisdiction of the Army's Provost Marshal General. A program to improve Army stockades by modernizing correctional programs and facilities and training correctional specialists was initiated. Enforcement aspects of the absentee problem were studied and apprehension procedures were reviewed. The Department of Justice's Crime Information Center provides support for the Army's apprehension program. Eventually this program will be automated and extended throughout the armed forces.

During the year ending November 30, 1968, there were 23,832 cases in which U.S. Army personnel were charged with offenses that were subject to the jurisdiction of foreign courts. In 9,114 of these cases, the offenses were subject to exclusive foreign jurisdiction because they involved only violations of foreign law. The remaining 14,718 cases involved alleged violations of both U.S. and foreign law, over which the foreign country had primary jurisdiction. This was waived in 13,865 (94 percent) of these cases. Of the 6,924 U.S. Army personnel tried by foreign courts, only 89 received sentences to confinement that were not suspended.

During 1969 the Army Claims Service processed 82,645 claims representing over $20 million in obligations against the U.S. government, and recovered over $1.3 million from carriers, warehousemen, insurers, and other third parties.

Dissent

The Army's problems are to some degree a reflection of the nation's problems. American youths bring into the Army the ideals, philosophies, and opinions of their society. The forms of dissent are numerous and varied, and the exercise of some of them, deliberate or otherwise, in the military environment would be prejudicial to good order and discipline.

In the summer of 1968 there were increasing indications that deliberate attempts were being made to undermine discipline and resist established authority. Press attention focused on the potential for disruption from within the Army. To investigate the general situation and co-ordinate and monitor information and actions related to Army morale and discipline, a special committee was established in August 1968.

The committee found that public manifestations of dissent spring from diverse undercurrents, ranging from the usual gripes of soldiers on through complaints of racial discrimination and up to politically motivated resistance to legally constituted authority. Actions have taken the form of refusal to obey orders, publication of so-called underground newspapers, soldier participation in antiwar meetings and demonstrations, and petitions in civil courts to establish the rights of soldiers.

Statistical yardsticks do not reveal a uniform magnitude to the threat. One determined soldier intent on spreading his personal philosophy by organizing others is not statistically significant, but he is a time-consuming nuisance to his unit leaders. The best estimates of the number of soldier organizers Army-wide place them at less than 100. Local commanders are responsible for handling individual cases; to assist them, a guidance letter was issued on May 28, 1969, outlining legally acceptable measures for dealing with dissidents and the tools of their trade.

Health and Medical Care

In fiscal year 1969, Army active duty personnel were admitted to hospitals and quarters at a rate of 376 per 1,000 average strength per year, slightly lower than the rate of 388 per 1,000 in 1968. The noneffective rate, representing the average daily number of Army personnel in an "excused from duty" status due to medical causes per 1,000 average strength, rose to 19.4 from 17.2 in the previous year. Noneffectiveness due to injuries resulting from hostile actions rose to 5.4 per 1,000 average strength from 4.5 in 1968.

The following table displays admission rates in Vietnam and other areas for all causes, and separately for all diseases and all injuries, along with incidence rates of malaria and certain other conditions which may cause a high proportion of noneffectiveness.

ADMISSIONS TO HOSPITALS AND QUARTERS AND INCIDENCE OF SELECTED
CONDITIONS—U.S. ARMY PERSONNEL ON ACTIVE DUTY
FISCAL YEAR 1969

(Rates per 1,000 average strength per year)

	World-wide	CONUS Army Areas	Oversea Area Total	Europe	Pacific	
					All Areas	Vietnam
Admissions						
All causes	376	364	389	248	452	508
Disease	311	334	285	216	312	336
Injury [1]	65	30	104	32	140	172
Incidence						
Malaria	7.92	2.39	14.01	0.24	20.98	24.72
Diarrheal diseases	19.89	12.23	28.31	14.59	33.39	38.28
Acute upper respiratory infection and influenza	110.70	165.60	50.33	62.10	41.85	37.66
Skin diseases, including dermatophytosis	9.06	5.38	13.12	3.80	17.66	21.03
Neuropsychiatric conditions	11.17	10.73	11.66	8.24	12.92	13.64
Hepatitis Viral	3.42	2.09	4.88	0.28	7.15	7.81

[1] Includes Army personnel wounded or injured as a result of actions of hostile forces.

Army hospitals in continental United States were severely taxed during the year as a result of a sustained increase in patients from the expanded combat in Vietnam and shortages in authorized staff. The staff deficit was aggravated by civilian hiring restrictions imposed by Public Law 90–364, passed in July 1968, and reductions in Army medical detachment spaces in CONUS general support forces effective in January 1969. As the year closed, there were indications that the restrictive situation would be alleviated by the addition of 4,725 medical spaces under 1970 strength authorizations, although training lead time would delay their full effectiveness until the second and third quarters of that fiscal year.

To reduce work load under the stringent conditions and protect the statutory entitlement of active duty personnel of the uniformed services to unqualified care, an Army policy letter was issued on March 12, 1969, outlining priorities for medical care. Of necessity this had adverse impact in some areas for retired personnel and dependents, whose entitlement to medical care had to be limited to a "when available" basis. Lower priority eligibles were referred to civilian sources under the Civilian Health and Medical Care Program of the Uniformed Services (CHAMPUS), generally at a higher cost to the individual than if the care had been provided in a military facility.

Over the past several years a Department of Defense working group has been developing an automated medical examination system that would incorporate the latest recording, evaluation, and analysis techniques. The purposes of the system would be to conserve manpower, increase the accuracy and quality of the examination, complete forms automatically, improve record storage and retrieval, provide statistical data for further evaluation as to the validity of the present examination, provide a more accurate base line upon which to evaluate change in an individual's physical condition, and do all of this economically. As executive agent for the Department of Defense in the operation of the Armed Forces examining and entrance stations (AFEES), the Army has chaired the working group and conducted a successful field test at the Philadelphia AFEES. The new system will be installed in all 74 examining stations.

The Military Blood Program Agency, a part of the Office of The Surgeon General, discharges all responsibilities and functions delegated to the Army for the conduct of the Department of Defense blood program. The agency receives requirements for whole blood and makes allocations among the armed services. The Army operates 17 blood donor centers, strategically located near large troop concentrations. It has provided over 52 percent of the blood needed in Southeast Asia; by June 30, 1969, 625,000 units of blood had been shipped there, almost double the amount supplied during the Korean War.

Housing, Safety, and Awards

Based on long-range strength and deployment estimates, Army requirements for family housing total 350,743 units. Available at permanent installations at year-end in military-controlled on- and off-post housing were 207,661 units. Progress in reducing the deficit will depend upon approval of Army budget requests for family housing construction and upon congressional funding.

There is also a substantial worldwide deficit in bachelor housing for both officers and enlisted men. About 32,874 new bachelor officer quarters (BOQ) spaces and 230,560 enlisted men's barracks spaces are required. Army personnel are still housed in obsolete World War II buildings at many locations. Efforts are under way to improve BOQ standards, but this will cost money in a period of heavy competing demands. To overcome the backlog in a reasonable period of time would require annual outlays of about $100 million for barracks construction and $25 million for BOQ's.

For the 21st time in the past 25 years, the Army received the National Safety Council's highest award for achievement, the Safety Award of Honor, this time for its record in accident prevention in fiscal year 1968. In turn, the Department of the Army presented its Award of Honor for Safety and Award of Merit for Safety to major commands, armies, and divisions for outstanding records in accident reduction. The Army safety program is designed to hold to a minimum the accidental loss of manpower, materiel, and monetary resources that retard efficiency and reduce the combat effectiveness of the Army. Major causes of accidental fatalities usually involve privately owned motor vehicles, aircraft, military vehicles, small arms, and drownings. Except for the first of these, the bulk of the problems were associated with activities in Vietnam.

In January 1969 the President established a Meritorious Service Medal to recognize noncombat meritorious service or achievement. The new medal joins the Distinguished Service Medal, Legion of Merit, and Army Commendation Medal in the peacetime award picture, serving as a counterpart to the Bronze Star Medal of wartime application.

Civilian Personnel

Army civilian personnel strength rose during fiscal year 1969 from 566,417 to 577,045. Except for the transfer of about 24,000 National Guard civilian technicians into the Army, this strength would have shown a slight decline. On an adjusted basis, the net decrease for the year was 2.4 percent, with the full-time permanent work force declining less than 1.7 percent. The citizen work force declined 3.8 percent; however, the local national work force increased by 1.3 percent due to an 18.1 percent increase in Southeast Asia. Direct hire employees this year outnumbered indirect hire employees for the first time since the oversea commands have used the indirect hire system.

Public Law 90–364, the Revenue and Expenditure Control Act of 1968, was signed on June 28, 1968, and became effective on July 1, 1968. One of its purposes was to reduce government expenditures by reducing the number of federal employees. The law prescribed that full-time employment in permanent positions be reduced to June 1966 levels, and that employment in temporary and part-time positions be restricted in any month to the number assigned in the same month of 1967. The reduction in full-time employment was to be accomplished by filling only 75 percent of vacancies created by separation after June 30, 1968.

The Army had 416,280 employees in full-time permanent military functions on June 30, 1968, compared with 340,991 on June 30, 1966. The bulk of the increase was due to the war in Vietnam and the civilianization program under which about 20,000 positions were converted from military to civilian occupancy. Some of the increase was due also to new and expanded missions approved by Congress.

The new law raised several problems in personnel management as well as in over-all operation of the Army. July, the month in which the law took effect, is a month of high intake, especially among college graduates who are hired to replace current and anticipated losses. Such personnel receive firm offers during the academic year preceding entry on duty, and the Army is legally obligated to honor such commitments. Long-range programs to attract highly qualified personnel suffered damage. Commanders were unable to respond to mission needs by shifting intake patterns, and were forced to readjust their civilian resources by mandatory reassignments and reductions in force, at a heavy price to civilian morale. Imbalances caused by a need to support high priority missions at levels substantially above that of June 30, 1966, caused inadequate staffing in other programs essential to Army operations.

The Army sought and was granted a measure of relief. As of October 1, 1968, the Army was authorized to exempt from the employment provision of the law those positions established after June 30, 1966, to support Southeast Asia operations and located in the theater. Similarly, teachers in the oversea dependent school program were exempted, and temporary and part-time ceilings for fiscal year 1969 were amended. But exemption of the civilianization program was denied, as was exemption for new programs like the Sentinel-Safeguard system.

Management of the Army's civilian work force under an arbitrary legal formula has created administrative problems that outweigh the advantages expected to be achieved under the law. Agencies with a high turnover were faced with continually reducing staffs without commensurate decreases in work load; this turnover was often an accident of geographical location and not a reflection of management skill. The formula also caused a skill imbalance, as agencies had no control over skill losses that occurred under the voluntary attrition program.

The Army managed to achieve its fiscal year 1969 reduction goal, but the full impact is difficult to measure, and there may be far-reaching consequences. For example, maintenance of equipment and facilities which had been performed on an austere basis during the Vietnam build-up has had to be further curtailed; minor projects will become major programs by the time resources can be diverted to them. Dollar savings resulting from the personnel cutback are a matter of record, but the debit side is unknown at the present time. The full impact on over-all Army mission accomplishment and on morale, motivation, and recruitment of the civilian work force is yet to be measured.

In the area of position and pay management, supergrade positions were reviewed in fiscal year 1969 and the Army worked with the Office of the Secretary of Defense and the Civil Service Commission in the development of grade structures, evaluation plans, regulations, and instructions concerning the Coordinated Federal Wage System. The position structure at all levels was kept under surveillance.

The Army has been the pioneer in the federal service in the establishment of a structured career management system. Although Army-wide activity began in earnest only in the early 1960's, programs are well established and operational and have served as forerunners for Defense-wide programs and information sources for other federal agencies, including the Civil Service Commission. Army civilian career programs are composed of key professional, managerial, or technical occupations. At the present time, more than 81,000 Army civilians in grades GS–5 through GS–18 are included in 14 Army-wide programs. The objectives of the program are to anticipate and meet continuing and future personnel needs with quality personnel while providing career opportunities that will attract and retain qualified employees.

In September 1968 the Civil Service Commission announced guidelines on a new federal promotion and internal placement policy. The Army's merit promotion program, already generally in line with the new policy, must conform fully by July 1, 1969. The more significant changes related to consideration, application, and testing of employees.

There was continuing active attention during the year to a battery of important personnel programs—the equal employment opportunity program; the federal women's program; the Youth Opportunity Campaign; Project Value, under which the disadvantaged in metropolitan areas are provided employment; employment of the handicapped; and the Vietnam era veterans employment referral program. The Civil Service Commission inspected the equal employment programs of some 70 Army installations during the year; women were increasingly employed in non-traditional and higher grade positions; over 18,000 youths were employed by the Army in the summer of 1968; the Army acquired responsibility for 13 metropolitan areas and employment of 1,350 disadvantaged workers under Project Value; a new honorary award was established to recognize outstanding contributions by handicapped employees; and the Army employed as civilians over 5,500 Vietnam veterans during calendar year 1968.

In November 1968 the Secretary of the Army approved the establishment of an award to recognize and encourage achievement and potential of young men and women who undertake a career in civilian personnel administration in the Army. Designated the William H. Kushnick Award in honor of the Army's Director of Civilian Personnel in World War II, the new award is presented for important achievements or contributions in civilian personnel administration within the department, or for outstanding performance in this field.

Both military and civilian personnel made valuable suggestions during the year that contributed to more economical and efficient operations. Under the Army suggestion program, 95,217 civilians (220 per 1,000 employees) submitted suggestions during fiscal year 1969, of which 28,138 were adopted, leading to first-year measurable benefits of close to $76.5 million. There were 47,158 suggestions from military personnel, and the 5,337 adopted will produce first-year measurable benefits in excess of $14.5 million.

Employee union activity increased in the fiscal year, although the pace was reduced from the two previous years. There are now 694 bargaining units in the Army—461 exclusive and 233 formal. The ratio of exclusive to formal units continues to increase each year, reflecting continued efforts by unions to obtain the right to negotiate labor-management agreements covering conditions of employment. At year-end there were 243 such agreements in force. The need to train top management officials, supervisors, and civilian personnel technicians in labor relations has grown, and 430 personnel attended seminars during the year.

The Army's U.S. citizen civilian employees overseas continued to provide specialized knowledge and expertise in logistic and support activities in various areas of the world. Attention was given to the rotation program under which career employees accepting foreign assignment agree to return within five years to a position in the United States. Army commands continued to rely heavily on indigenous employees in various host countries for various skills. Although local national wages and benefits continued to rise in all countries during the year, the payroll cost of a local national remained considerably below the cost if importing a U.S. citizen civilian to fill a job. Foreign commands continued to conduct training programs to develop the capability of indigenous personnel.

V. Reserve Forces

The Army's Reserve Component mission is to prepare individuals and units to augment the active Army in times of emergency. To carry it out, the Army develops mobilization and contingency plans and programs for utilization of National Guard and Reserve elements. In fiscal year 1969 this responsibility was shaped by the partial mobilization required by the war in Vietnam and by the stimulations, preparations, and adjustments that attend a contingency period.

Partial Mobilization of the Reserve Components

The Reserve Component reorganization and the limited mobilization of Army National Guard (ARNG) and U.S. Army Reserve (USAR) units, accomplished in the closing months of fiscal year 1968, set the tempo for 1969. Postmobilization training was completed in August and October by the 76 units mobilized on May 13, 1968. Of these units, 43 were deployed to Vietnam in the period August–December 1968, and 33 became a part of the Army's Strategic Reserve. In addition, approximately 2,700 members of the U.S. Army Reserve were ordered to active duty from the Individual Ready Reserve.

The 1968 mobilization, although limited, served its purpose well. Essential units were provided to meet requirements in Vietnam and in the Strategic Army Forces significantly earlier than would have been possible had active Army units been formed, trained, and equipped.

Plans were developed late in the fiscal year for the release of the mobilized units. They will be restored to state or Army area command control by mid-December 1969. To insure their logistical support, equipment on hand was allocated for their use and a funding program was developed to meet further equipment and supply needs at the time of demobilization.

By law the Army Reserve Component's average strengths for fiscal year 1969 were set at 400,000 for the Army National Guard and 260,000 for the Army Reserve. These over-all strengths were required to be reduced by the strength of the mobilized units. Thus at the close of fiscal year 1969, Reserve Component paid drill strength totaled 650,276 (388,954 ARNG; 261,322 USAR). Enlisted accessions during the year totaled 105,038 (50,454 ARNG; 54,584 USAR), including 91,607 nonprior-service personnel (43,096 ARNG; 48,511 USAR). Paid drill strength was distributed as follows:

Component	Officers	Enlisted	Total
ARNG	30,432	358,522	388,954
USAR	32,218	229,104	261,322
Total	62,650	587,626	650,276

At the beginning of the year there were 18,426 (8,239 ARNG; 10,187 USAR) nonprior-service enlistees awaiting initial active duty for training for a period of at least four months under the reserve enlistment program. Of 69,500 (32,600 ARNG; 36,900 USAR) individuals programed to enter active duty for training, only 67,472 (31,290 ARNG; 36,182 USAR) entered, due to lack of training spaces. Enlisted men awaiting initial active duty training on June 30, 1969, totaled 41,029 (19,377 ARNG; 21,652 USAR).

During the year, 1,628 (780 ARNG; 848 USAR) individuals were ordered to active duty for failure to participate in required training.

At the beginning of the fiscal year there were 2,193 (1,659 ARNG; 534 USAR) assigned aviators on flying status in the Reserve Components. At year-end this had dropped to 2,191 (1,640 ARNG; 551 USAR). A lack of quotas for primary aviator training continued to make it difficult to replace losses from normal attrition.

Training and Readiness

The attained Reserve Component strength supports the basic structure created by the organization that was completed in May 1968. That structure is outlined on the chart below.

RESERVE COMPONENT UNIT STRUCTURE

	ARNG	USAR	Total
Combat divisions	8	0	8
Training divisions	0	13	13
Combat brigades	18	3	21
Military police battalions	7	4	11
Maneuver area commands	0	2	2
Air defense battalions	31	0	31
Field army support command	0	1	1
Support brigades	1	4	5
Adjutant general units	40	121	161
Civil affairs units	0	53	53
Composite service units	123	163	286
Finance units	1	26	27
JAG units	0	226	226
PSYOPS units	0	6	6
Hospital units	15	106	121
Garrison units	0	9	9
Public information units	34	24	58
Terminal units	0	19	19
Total companies and detachments	[1][2] 2,898	[1] 3,477	[1][2] 6,375

[1] Includes the following units mobilized May 13, 1968:
    ARNG—83 companies and detachments
    USAR—45 companies and detachments
    Total—128 companies and detachments
[2] Does not include ARNG companies and detachments organized for the sole purpose of satisfying state needs, and for which equipment procurement is not authorized.

Eight more ARNG units were authorized for fiscal year 1969 than in the previous year. Although some NIKE-HERCULES units were deleted from the structure, they were replaced, and over-all strength was maintained by the addition of some transportation, military police, and engineer units.

Reserve component readiness improved during the year. Since certain units were deleted from the Reserve structure in the reorganization for which no contingency requirements were foreseen, there was no further need for the selected reserve force (SRF) as a separate entity in the force structure. The SRF designation will be terminated on September 30, 1969.

A revised Army regulation (AR 135-8), entitled "The Reserve Component Unit Readiness Report," was published on March 10, 1969. It establishes uniform readiness standards and reporting procedures, and the readiness report—the first since 1966—will be prepared semiannually as of April 30 and October 31, and will incorporate data to identify general constraints to the attainment of readiness posture.

Army National Guard and U.S. Army Reserve training attendance and participation remained at high levels during the year, as indicated below.

PERCENT OF PARTICIPATION

Fiscal Year	ARNG	USAR
1967	95.8	88.3
1968	97.3	91.8
1969	96.9	91.5

While Reserve Component forces continued to meet minimum training standards, there were shortages of certain kinds of equipment that inhibited progress. Efforts to insure that available resources are used to the maximum produced improvements.

The general training objective for Reserve Component units in the 1968–69 training year was to complete platoon-level schedules and conduct platoon tests during annual field training in the summer of 1969. Artillery units will complete battery-level testing in the same period. The objective had been generally achieved by year-end, with some units conducting training successfully at one or two levels above the established minimum standards.

During fiscal year 1969, the director for civil disturbance planning and operations conducted a detailed analysis of the over-all force requirements for the control of possible simultaneous civil disorders. As a result of this analysis, the number of USAR brigades assigned civil disturbance missions was reduced from 69 to 18 (3 TOE and 15 provisional). These organizations received specialized training to increase their state of preparedness to perform this mission.

All Army National Guard combat, combat support, and combat service support units whose missions include support of civil authorities were authorized to participate in up to four unit training assemblies in civil disturbance operations in the year. This refresher training, undertaken at the expense of the primary mission, improved the Army's and the state's capability to cope with civil disturbances.

National Guard personnel continued to attend Army service and area schools—9,115 officers and enlisted personnel in the year. Five hundred and seventy-five senior Guard commanders and 244 USAR members attended the senior officers civil disturbance orientation course at the Military Police School, Fort Gordon, Georgia, and about 300 ARNG technicians attended special training courses on new types of equipment such as the M–715 truck. Enrollment in the state Officer Candidate School program was curtailed to insure that all graduates would be commissioned; the states restricted input to about 3,000, including almost 300 USAR candidates, and about 1,800 were to graduate during the summer of 1969.

Enrollment in U.S. Army Reserve schools for school year 1968–69 increased by 29.3 percent over that of May 1968, including both officer and enlisted categories. Over 12,200 were enrolled in branch officer advanced courses and command and general staff courses, an increase of about 17.8 percent over enrollments in May 1968. This figure will increase beginning in the fall of 1969 when the branch officer course enters the formal U.S. Army Reserve school curriculum. Over-all, a total of 11,584 Army Reserve officers and enlisted men attended Army service and area schools in the year.

Materiel and Supply

The reorganization of the Reserve Component force structure in fiscal year 1968 required a redistribution of equipment, and this was substantially completed in fiscal year 1969. Over 16,000 items had to be redistributed. In general, the equipment status of the Reserve Components improved during the year, the result of higher priorities for repair parts to maintain equipment. Additional funds were available for depot maintenance on certain tanks, guns, and trucks. In fiscal year 1969 the Reserve Components received about $1.2 million in depot maintenance support from the Army Materiel Command.

The Reserve Components both received and lost some major equipment items. Received were M–109 self-propelled howitzers, M–151A1 ¼-ton trucks, 12-ton semitrailer vans, 5,000-gallon semitrailer tank trucks, 5-ton dump trucks, and industrial tractors with scrapers. Certain other items were withdrawn for active Army use.

Facilities

The suspension on Reserve Component military construction was lifted in February 1968. Although some individual projects were approved in fiscal year 1968, the fiscal year 1969 military construction programs for Reserve Components represented the initial program package submitted and approved subsequent to the lifting of the suspension and the reorganization.

The Army National Guard carried over $16.4 million in prior-year construction funds (MCARNG). Coupled with a new obligation authority of $2.7 million for fiscal year 1969, funding in the amount of $19.1 million was available to support the fiscal year 1969 MCARNG program. The Army Reserve carried over $11.5 million from prior-year construction funds (MCAR) which, coupled with $3 million in new obligation authority, provided $14.5 million to support the fiscal year 1969 MCAR program.

The fiscal year 1969 budget plan provided $9.5 million for Army National Guard military construction and $9 million for the Army Reserve. The MCARNG project approvals included 20 armory and 15 nonarmory projects. The MCAR approvals provided 11 USAR centers and 1 center expansion. Two of these centers are to be jointly constructed with the U.S. Navy.

In July 1968, subsequent to the reorganization, the Reserve Components began a comprehensive evaluation of current facilities and known requirements from which to develop a long-range facilities plan. The current Reserve Components real property inventory is valued at $870.6 million (ARNG $632.4 million; USAR $238.2). The Reserve Components occupied 3,793 Army-type facilities (2,774 ARNG; 1,019 USAR), of which 2,003 were constructed with federal funds or federal contributions to the states, 492 are leased or licensed, and 1,298 donated or permitted.

Based upon the results of the study, requirements were determined and program change requests submitted for a 10-year long-range plan with fiscal year 1970 as the initial construction year. Subsequent program change decisions for fiscal year 1970 and the Five Year Defense Plan led to a proposed 15-year program costing $25 million annually in fiscal years 1970 and 1971 and $30 million annually in the remaining years.

In March 1969, the Secretary of Defense requested a revalidation of long-range construction requirements and establishment of a balanced 10-year construction program.

Program change requests have been submitted for the Army National Guard and the Army Reserve. Based upon current costs, $627.3 million is required for needed construction. Of this amount, $299.3 million is for MCARNG and $328 million for the MCAR.

Air Defense

At the beginning of fiscal year 1969, the Army National Guard air defense program consisted of 1 group headquarters, 17 battalion headquarters, and 54 fire units located in 17 states. During the year, the Defense Department announced the closeout of three headquarters and headquarters batteries and seven firing batteries. The remaining units represent all of the NIKE-HERCULES missile defense for Hawaii and a significant percentage of the NIKE-HERCULES units of the U.S. Army Air Defense Command. These units, manned by approximately 4,800 ARNG technicians, are located to protect selected population and industrial centers against air attack and are operational around the clock. In fiscal year 1969, these ARNG units enjoyed the best operational performance record since entering the air defense program in 1952.

Management

During fiscal year 1969 a special board met to consider ways of managing the Army's Reserve Component officer corps more effectively. The board recommended the development of a career management and personnel management system for Reserve Component officers; development of a record monitoring system to improve personnel management control; a comprehensive officer acquisition and distribution system; development of standards for promotion and federal recognition; clear and equitable general officer promotion criteria; and development of the most effective system possible for guiding and monitoring training in the Reserve Components. As the year closed some of the recommendations had been implemented and others were being worked on.

Most of the Reserve Components units were converted to the new Army Authorization Documents System during 1969. Generally, like units will have common tables of organization and equipment and tables of allowances. Standardization will promote uniformity in units and facilitate personnel assignment and management.

Automatic data processing support for the Reserve Components was transferred from the U.S. Army Data Support Command and the U.S. Army Management Systems Support Command to the U.S. Army Administration Center at St. Louis, Missouri, on February 1, 1969.

There were two other personnel management developments in the year that deserve mention. A new Army National Guard automated personnel reporting system was implemented with the collection of an individual officer master tape record at the bureau level and an individual enlisted card deck at the state level. The command sergeant major program, already in operation in the active Army, was extended to the Reserve Components in 1969, a move to improve the caliber and effectiveness of the enlisted men who hold the most responsible position in the Reserve Components.

Support to Civil Authorities

During the year 52,524 National Guardsmen were called by their governors to state active duty in civil disturbance emergencies. They were committed 56 times in 21 states to assist local authorities to quell disturbances in cities and on college campuses. In no instance was it necessary for a governor to request federal assistance. The Guard had conducted refresher riot control training, and additional special riot control equipment had been issued. Most states also had conducted civil disturbance command post exercises in conjunction with local and state civil authorities. Senior Guard commanders and planners, as noted earlier, attended a civil disturbance orientation course at the Military Police School, and civilian law enforcement officers also attended the same course, in many instances at the same time as their local National Guard commander. Thus the Guard's ability to cope with civil disturbances was considerably improved, as demonstrated in its utilization in this regard.

In addition to civil disturbance assignment, National Guard elements were called to state active duty by 19 governors to assist civil authorities in natural disasters and other public emergencies. There were blizzards, floods, fires, train and aircraft accidents, tornadoes, and power failures that required Guard assistance in snow removal, dike patrol, traffic control, evacuation of refugees, protection of property, searches for missing persons and aircraft, and prison security during guard strikes, among other tasks.

States have been issued special civil disturbance control equipment. They are also completing their procurement of single sideband transceiver radios; these radios, both fixed station and mobile, have been a tremendous asset to states not only during emergencies but in day-to-day communications.

Technicians

At the beginning of the year, 4,467 technicians supplied administrative and maintenance support for USAR units. This dropped to 4,357 by year-end as the U.S. Army Reserve complied with the provisions of Public Law 90–364, which required personnel reductions to the levels of June 30, 1966 (see ch. 4), when technician program strength was 4,028. Attrition was to be accomplished by filling only 70 percent of losses. The Army reduced this to 35 percent for the months of March through May 1969. Thus the USAR lost 578 spaces out of a budgetary authorization of 5,045, and an additional 110 spaces through attrition.

Prior to enactment of the National Guard Technicians Act of 1968 (Public Law 90–486, 82 stat. 755), which became effective on January 1, 1969, National Guard technicians were considered to be state employees (*Maryland for the use of Levin et. al.* v. *U.S.* 381, *U.S.* 41 [1965]). Technicians covered by state retirement systems on the date of enactment of the cited act were permitted to elect between continuation of that coverage or the retirement legislation applying to federal employees. Under the latter, however, National Guard technician service before January 1969 is reduced by 45 percent in computing retirement annuity.

ARNG technician strength was 23,740 as the fiscal year opened and 24,211 as it closed.

VI. Management, Budget, and Funds

The Army's management mission consists of continuing actions to plan, organize, direct, co-ordinate, control, and evaluate the use of men, money, materials, and facilities to accomplish missions and tasks. Its budgetary mission consists of determining how much money is required to carry out Army responsibilities, and its funding mission consists of allocating that money for specific purposes. In fiscal year 1969 these functions were shaped by the war in Vietnam, the Army's worldwide commitment, and the need to make the most effective use of all resources in a period of heavy expenditures, inflationary pressures, and competing demands.

Organizational Developments

The increasing development and installation of automatic data processing systems to support functional applications that may be similar in two or more major Army commands raised a need for better central planning and control. To satisfy that need, the U.S. Army Computer Systems Command (USACSC) was activated at Fort Belvoir, Virginia, on March 31, 1969. The command was designated a class II activity under the jurisdiction of the Assistant Vice Chief of Staff. It was assigned responsibility for development, installation, improvement, and other related support functions for Army multicommand automatic data processing systems, and will perform project management for assigned systems in response to functional requirements formulated by headquarters staff agencies. The command will insure effective communications planning and support for such systems and will conduct software research programs in co-ordination with the Chief of Research and Development.

Late in fiscal year 1968 the Directorate of Management Information Systems in the Office of the Assistant Vice Chief of Staff completed a study which revealed that certain organizational realignments at Headquarters, Department of the Army, level would benefit the Army's approach to information systems design and promote a more effective use of automatic data processing equipment. Thus in July 1968 the responsibilities assigned to the Director of Automatic Data Processing in the Office of the Comptroller of the Army were transferred to the management information systems directorate, including jurisdiction over the Computer Systems Evaluation Command. The latter was redesignated as the Computer Systems Support and Evaluation Command and was made a class II activity under the directorate. As a result of this realignment, the management information systems directorate is now able to monitor, on an Army-wide basis, the design of information systems and the use of associated automatic data processing equipment. The directorate also has the professional capability to evaluate and select computers for all elements of the Army and provide a single point of contact with industry in this field.

In August 1968 the Chief of Staff directed that the Family Housing Division, Office of the Chief of Engineers, be transferred to the Office of the Deputy Chief of Staff for Logistics (ODCSLOG). This action was the result of a Department of the Army study to insure that the family housing program is organized and executed in a manner commensurate with its importance to the welfare and morale of married Army personnel. As a result of the transfer the Director of Installations, ODCSLOG, is the Family Housing Programs and Appropriations Director and is the principal Department of the Army witness on family housing matters before congressional committees.

In the area of facilities management, the Chief of Staff assigned the Deputy Chief of Staff for Logistics over-all responsibility for the design, development, and subsequent management of an integrated facilities system, and directed the development of a staff organization to carry out this responsibility. On September 21, 1968, establishment of the Integrated Facilities System Office under the Director of Installations was approved.

In July 1968 the mission responsibilities of the Special Assistant for Logistical Support of Army Aircraft and the Special Assistant for Logistical Support of Tactical Communications were expanded to the extent that redesignations were necessary to describe more appropriately their respective areas of responsibility. The Office of the Special Assistant for Logistical Support of Army Aircraft was redesignated the Aviation Logistics Management Office, and the Special Assistant for Logistical Support of Tactical Communications was redesignated the Special Assistant for Logistical Support of Communications-Electronics.

Management Programs, Systems, and Techniques

The purpose of resource related planning is to assist the Chief of Staff in programing the allocation of Army resources in the light of probable future budget constraints. Two major tasks are budget projection and allocation of funds to alternative uses. The Assistant Vice Chief of Staff early in 1969 established a working group to project Army budgets 10 years into the future and to develop a management system to assess the effects of future constrained budgets on the force development and weapon selection process. Budget projections are extrapolated from economic growth trends and historic budget levels, assuming a constant baseline force. The original hand-operated resource allocation model is being automated. When this automation is completed, it will be possible to assess quickly the effects on future Army budgets of varying weapon modernization rates, force readiness levels, and theater of operation equipment priorities. The increased visibility of Army programs gained through this approach should permit more direct and timely guidance to the Army staff concerning weapon system and force composition issues.

During fiscal year 1969 the first phase of the resource management system, Project PRIME, was implemented. Under this application, attention was centered on expenses as a means of managing resources. Under the new procedures, military personnel costs were figured on the basis of grade rates, appropriations were realigned to differentials between expenses and investments, the approved operating budget was used to issue financial authorizations, and accrual methods were used to account for financial resources.

The second phase of the Program to Improve Management of Army Resources (PRIMAR) was conducted during the period January 1968– May 1969. The study examined the Army resource management system with the objective of improving the efficiency of Army planning, programing, and budgeting activities. Specific results of the study include (1) a proposed readiness measurement system consisting of displays which can provide improved management of forces, personnel, and equipment programs in meeting specific readiness goals; (2) a revised Army planning system to assist the Army in providing better force and resource recommendations to the Joint Chiefs of Staff (JCS) and the Office of the Secretary of Defense (OSD); (3) improved programing processes to permit design of resource programs which balance with prescribed force structures and readiness levels; and (4) a guidance package to improve the communications of objectives, missions, and resource allocations to subordinate commands.

Implementation of the study recommendations is under way but, due to the wide variation in the state of development of various subsystems, installation into a fully operational system will require several years. Under the monitorship and guidance of the Assistant Vice Chief of Staff, the separate subsystems are becoming operational but require continual adjustment to insure that the over-all system is fully integrated and is responsive to the requirements of OSD, JCS, and top-level Army management.

The structure and composition system (SACS) is the Army's large-scale automated computational system. It consists of 137 computer programs and is used to generate line item authorization data for all units. SACS uses the force accounting system (FAS) file and matches the selected force with appropriate authorization files to generate authorization data.

To date, SACS has been used over 50 times in major requirements computations. It was used to develop equipment requirements for the President's Budget, the 1970 budget estimate and apportionment, posthostilities force planning, and development of the Army Force Development Plan. SACS has also been of assistance in estimating personnel requirements and has proved useful in staff studies, estimates, and plans, including input to the Joint Strategic Operations Plan, OSD manpower reports, limited war reserve studies, and personnel high interest skill summaries.

To enhance further the effectiveness of the Army's basic resource management systems, a committee of general officers was established in May 1969. The committee, named the Keystone Management Systems Steering Committee, is chaired by the Assistant Vice Chief of Staff. Its main objective is to examine the Army's keystone authorization and asset reporting systems, to assure that they are responsive to managers' requirements at all levels.

In fiscal year 1968 the Army conducted a Study of Management Information Systems Support (SOMISS) to determine how Army operation in this increasingly active and important field could be improved. A number of recommendations were developed and were approved in July 1968. The study concluded that the departmental headquarters organization for managing automated data processing systems should be strengthened, and this was done with the creation of the Computer Systems Command and the organizational realignments described above. The SOMISS finding that a separate design agency for automatic data processing (ADP) systems be created and that departmental technical support to users be broadened was also inherent in that realignment, and during the year other steps were taken to carry out a recommendation that staff agency personnel in the various functional areas be made responsible for the functional design of automated systems in their respective fields. In conjunction with the SOMISS study, development began on a master plan for the entire complex of Army computer-based information systems. The first phase of this project was completed in December 1968 with the publication of an interim plan for the Army Management Information System under which guidance was issued for systems development, planning, procedures, and schedules for the first master plan due in September 1969.

As a primary step toward the development of a cohesive and usable logistics management information system, the Army has conducted a design project supported by the Stanford Research Institute. The objective is to establish an integrated supply, maintenance, and materiel readiness reporting system from the unit level up through intervening echelons to Headquarters, Department of the Army. Phase I of the study identified the essential elements of information required for management and decision-making at each echelon of the Army. Phase II covered design of the structure, organization, procedures, management indicators, and the data base for management at each echelon. The concept provides for the collection, processing, and storage of management data and output to management at all echelons. It has been designed to obtain this information from data banks supporting the horizontal operating system under development. Data bank input will come from reporting units in a "tap the source once" concept of reporting. It is the Army's intention that this effort will result in a standard worldwide information and operating system which will integrate supply, maintenance, and materiel readiness reporting into a single cohesive system which is vertically and horizontally integrated. Vertically it is integrated from Headquarters, Department of the Army, through all intervening echelons down to the operating unit level through the use of a uniform set of logistical management indicators, a minimum number of essential elements of information, and uniform reporting formats. It is designed so that only a relatively few selected key logistical management indicators and data elements flow from a given logistical management level to the next higher echelon of supervision. The selected indicators and data which flow upward are designed to give the supervising echelon a measurement of the over-all effectiveness of performance and variations from standards at the next lower level. The capability will exist, when required, of providing relevant detailed data from any echelon, from the lowest to the highest.

Horizontal integration is accomplished at each operating support and logistical control level by the use of the selected indicators and data tailored to satisfy the operating and management control requirements at each level. Reporting at each level will be on the "management by exception" principle, reporting to the commander only inadequate performance. Deficiencies will be pinpointed to identify the operating elements concerned and the specific logistic functional performance deficiencies requiring correction.

This concept will change the operating system now existing in the Army or currently under development, by introducing the selected indicators and data which are the salient characteristics of the integrated management information system. This is a first step in obtaining effective interface with the operating system, since management information can only be a product of the operating system and data base.

The final report on this 2-year design program has been co-ordinated with the Army staff and major commands. These comments were evaluated and were being given a final project advisory group review as the year closed.

The role of the auditor in Army management is no longer limited to the area of finance and accounts; the principal purpose of today's internal auditing is to appraise the effectiveness of management—that is, the Army auditor functions as in-house management consultant, an instrument of Army management.

During fiscal year 1969 the departmental staff and major commanders, as well as higher authority, placed increasing reliance on auditing as a means of analyzing Army systems, reviewing Army management controls, and evaluating the use of Army resources. Whereas in fiscal year 1965 the Army Audit Agency devoted most of its effort to periodic audit of Army installations, activities, and commands, in fiscal year 1969 the agency used over half of its resources to perform Army-wide and commandwide audits and to provide special audit services requested by higher authority.

Because of increasing demands for these services, the Army Staff Audit Priority Committee was established to assist in insuring that audit effort is devoted to management areas of greatest importance to the Army. As a result, the Army's scheduled audit program for fiscal year 1970, in addition to audits of installations, will concern itself with a variety of subjects of major interest to the Army, including authorization documents, trained enlisted replacements, industrial plant equipment, communications security logistics, stock fund operations, depot maintenance, cost reduction savings, and research and development.

The Army Audit Agency also increased its permanent staff and extended its activities in Vietnam. Originally confined to the Saigon area, Army auditors moved out to the base camps and support enclaves all the way from the Central Highlands to the Mekong Delta. Concentrating their attention on evaluations which could be accomplished within short periods and which offered immediate returns to command action, Army auditors provided valuable assistance to commanders in such areas as ammunition management and accounting, requisition processing, control over receipt and distribution of materiel, depot operations, property disposal, and personnel management.

The development, installation, and use of accrual accounting principles and procedures by all federal departments and agencies have been required by statute for more than a decade. During fiscal year 1969, the stimulus provided by recommendations of the President's Commission on Budget Concepts and implementing directives issued by the Bureau of the Budget and the Treasury Department have resulted in significant progress in this area. Policies and procedures for accounting and reporting of accrued expenditures and revenues on a test basis became effective July 1, 1968. It is anticipated that the improved procedures for fiscal year 1970 will provide a reliable base of data on accrued expenditures and revenues in support of the first accrual-based budget to be submitted for the budget year 1972.

The Army for the sixth year participated in the Defense Integrated Management Engineering Systems (DIMES) project to develop engineered time standards wherever possible. To date, about 70 percent of the potential personnel spaces in installations of the Army Materiel Command and Military Traffic Management and Terminal Service have been covered by performance standards. Favorable progress under DIMES had resulted in extension of its concepts to 165 activities by the close of the fiscal year, and about $55 million had been saved in Army installations up to June 30, 1969.

In the past fiscal year the Department of Defense has intensified emphasis on the interservice logistic support program as a means of effecting economies among the services. To this end each of the military services has designated an agency within its headquarters to serve as a central point of contact with responsibility for administering the program servicewide. The Deputy Chief of Staff for Logistics was so designated for the Army. The program has also been the subject of a comprehensive survey by the General Accounting Office, both within the continental United States and overseas, indicating that still greater emphasis may be expected during fiscal year 1970.

During the past year the Army commercial and industrial activities program has received increasing scrutiny from congressional committees, the General Accounting Office, the Civil Service Commission, the Bureau of the Budget, and such diverse nongovernmental groups as employee organizations and trade unions. In response to the heightened interest, the Army commercial and industrial activities program was redefined and revitalized. Management controls were strengthened and personnel assigned to the program at Headquarters, Department of the Army, on a full-time basis.

Budget and Funds

In fiscal year 1969 the President submitted to Congress a national budget totaling $186,062 million. The Revenue and Expenditure Control Act, which became effective on the opening day of the fiscal year, reduced the budget by $6 billion. The Department of Defense's share of this expenditure reduction was $3 billion, the Army's share $900 million.

The Army had requested $31,363.8 million in new obligational authority in its fiscal year 1969 budget request. In the President's Budget this was reduced to $25,214.6 million. The Congress in turn reduced this by appropriating $23,769.3 million, and a 1969 supplemental appropriation of $1,222.8 million led to a final fiscal year 1969 Army budget totaling $24,992.1 million.

To meet the $900 million expenditure reduction imposed on the Army, it was necessary, because of the time lag between obligation and payment, to reduce obligational authority by $1,472.7 million. Of this amount, Congress reduced the appropriation by $1,468.9 million, while the Office of the Secretary of Defense and the Army reduced the $3.8 million difference. To offset the reduction in part, Congress authorized a transfer of $60 million in cash from the Defense Supply Agency stock fund, which had not been requested in the President's Budget. Thus the effective obligational authority reduction was $1,412.7 million, with the associated expenditure reduction of $900 million.

The following table traces the fiscal year 1969 Army budget through its various stages.

DEPARTMENT OF THE ARMY
CHRONOLOGY OF THE BUDGET ESTIMATE, FISCAL YEAR 1969
NEW OBLIGATIONAL AUTHORITY

(In millions of dollars)

	Department of the Army	President's Budget	Appropriated PL 90-580	Supplemental Appropriation 1969 PL 91-47	Total Fiscal Year 1969
Military personnel, Army	8,541.7	8,136.0	8,000.0	375.0	8,375.0
Reserve personnel, Army	335.6	303.4	287.2	----------	287.2
National Guard personnel, Army	369.2	321.3	304.5	16.4	320.9
Operation and maintenance, Army	9,189.8	8,205.0	7,805.0	181.3	7,986.3
Operation and maintenance, ARNG	304.5	267.0	264.7	11.5[1]	276.2
National Board for the Promotion of Rifle Practice	0.4	----------	----------	----------	----------
Procurement of equipment and missiles, Army	8,573.6	5,626.0	5,031.4	640.1	5,671.5
Research, development, test, and evaluation, Army	2,073.8	1,661.9	1,522.7	−1.5[1]	1,521.2
Subtotal, excluding construction	29,388.6	24,520.6	23,215.4	1,222.8	24,438.3
			PL 90-513		
Military construction, Army	1,947.8	688.3	548.1	----------	548.1
Military construction, USAR	12.9	3.0	3.0	----------	3.0
Military construction, ARNG	14.4	2.7	2.7	----------	2.7
Subtotal, construction accounts	1,975.2	694.0	553.8	----------	553.8
Total NOA	31,363.8	25,214.6	23,769.3	1,222.8	24,992.1

[1] $1.5 million transferred from research, development, test, and evaluation to operation and maintenance, ARNG.
Note: May not add due to rounding.

Further streamlining in the Department of Defense management system occurred in 1969. The number of Draft Presidential Memoranda (DPM) were reduced from 16 to 3 and a new document, the major program memorandum (MPM), was introduced as a replacement for certain DPM's. Over-all, the number of Draft Presidential Memoranda, major program memoranda, and Defense Guidance Memoranda (DGM) was reduced from 20 to 12. Issue dates for this reduced number of documents were generally advanced in recognition of their relationship to the budget cycle. The advanced schedule allows more time to consider these documents and make decisions based on them in advance of submission of the budget. MPM are supported by resource annexes—an innovation that marked the 1969 cycle. These annexes are designed to facilitate the identification of the impact that MPM have on the Five Year Defense Program. In addition to the changes in DPM, MPM, and DGM outlined above, additional planning to improve even further the Department of Defense management and program systems was initiated in 1969. This planning addressed procedure, format, and the role of the JCS in the decision-making process as opposed to the role of the Office of the Secretary of Defense staff exemplified by the document cycle outlined above.

Cost Reduction

The Army continued its efforts to encourage greater efficiency and economy in all aspects of Army activity under the cost reduction program. An outstanding unit award was established in August 1968 to recognize the over-all excellence of a unit's cost reduction program, as well as its noteworthy savings accomplishments. The U.S. Army Infantry Center, Fort Benning, Georgia (Continental Army Command), was selected by the Office of the Secretary of Defense, along with units from the other military departments and the Defense Supply Agency, to receive an outstanding unit award presented by the President of the United States during cost reduction week ceremonies. Initial nominations for this award were made to the Department of the Army by the major Army commands on the basis of the subordinate unit's fiscal year 1968 accomplishments.

Army recognition was extended to other command nominees that met the Office of the Secretary of Defense award criteria but were not selected: Red River Army Depot, Texarkana, Texas (U.S. Army Materiel Command); Seventh Army Support Command (U.S. Army, Europe); 25th Transportation Center (U.S. Army, Pacific); 115th Military Intelligence Group, Presidio of San Francisco (U.S. Army Intelligence Corps); Headquarters, 40th Artillery Brigade, Presidio of San Francisco (U.S. Army Air Defense Command); and the U.S. Army Combat Developments Command Experimentation Command, Fort Ord, California (U.S. Army Combat Developments Command).

Progress in the cost reduction program continued during fiscal year 1969, when $379.4 million was saved against a goal of $263 million. The actions taken in the fiscal year are estimated to have a 3-year savings effect of $792.8 million for fiscal years 1969–71 against a goal of $525 million. The following examples are illustrative of field participation in the program.

A special study of the order and shipping time for individual combat meals, made by the 1st Logistical Command, Vietnam, resulted in reducing the days of supply in the pipeline from 180 to 165, with 1-time savings of $1,637,400 realized for fiscal year 1969.

A value engineering study conducted by the U.S. Army Engineer District, Savannah, Georgia, resulted in the modification of design requirements for the construction of the Fort Jackson Hospital, Columbia, South Carolina. Rather than requiring that the high rise portion be structurally completed prior to beginning construction of the low portions of the hospital, the change permits simultaneous construction of both portions—except for the bays connecting the two, which will be constructed after structure settlement has occurred. The resulting 8- to 10-month reduction in construction time produced savings of $328,800.

Military Pay System

As a part of the OSD program to reduce gold flow expenditures, the services were requested to consider the possibility of withdrawing the military pay function from oversea areas and administering it from a CONUS location. The original memorandum concerning this subject was dated May 3, 1967. At that time, the Army's position was that the desired reduction could be accomplished by the implementation of the Joint Uniform Military Pay System (JUMPS-Army).

On May 29, 1968, a memorandum was received from the Office of the Assistant Secretary of Defense (Comptroller) requesting that the Army again consider the possibility of a centralized pay record procedure. This request was prompted by the Air Force's success along this line and an apparent delay in the implementation of JUMPS-Army. The Army's response to this memorandum indicated that a plan would be developed to accomplish the desired relocation of military pay administration.

A conceptual plan for the subject relocation was developed which envisioned the establishment of a military pay service center for oversea areas (MPSCOA) at the U.S. Army Finance Center, Fort Benjamin Harrison, Indiana. The service center would maintain pay records for all members stationed in oversea areas. Additionally, the plan called for a test of the concept using the units in Europe currently being paid by JUMPS-Army. The test phase of the plan was approved for implementation in November 1968.

Pay clerks of the 44th Finance Section (Disbursing) involved in pay record maintenance and computation were relocated to the MPSCOA on March 15, 1969. Pay clerks from the 3d Infantry Division arrived in mid-April 1969. With these two segments as a base, the concepts outlined in the basic plan will be tested for a period of six months. At that time an evaluation will be made to determine whether further expansion in Europe and in other oversea areas is warranted.

As a part of the plan, it was determined that a communications system that would link finance offices in Europe with the MPSCOA was a necessity. Such a system was established for the units involved in the test. Evaluation of the concepts and the communications will determine the feasibility and desirability of administering the oversea military pay system at a central location in the continental United States.

VII. Logistics

The Army's logistics mission embraces materiel, personnel, facilities, and services. To carry it out, the Army must acquire, move, distribute, maintain, store, and dispose of materiel; move and support personnel; acquire, construct, operate, maintain, and dispose of facilities; and furnish services. In fiscal year 1969 the over-all task was generally shaped by the war in Vietnam and the Army's million-and-a-half strength and worldwide deployment. Once again efforts were directed toward achieving a balance between the requirements of the war, the support of Army forces elsewhere, and the general progress in long-range programs so essential to future readiness and deterrence.

Procurement

For the past decade the procurement objectives for materiel support of general purpose forces have been set out by the Secretary of Defense in his annual logistics guidance. The guidance establishes a balance between programed forces and the equipment, ammunition, secondary items, and consumables required to sustain them in combat. It specifies the number of Army division forces to be equipped and supported, and the Army's budget is developed accordingly.

In fiscal year 1969 the budget for the procurement of equipment and missiles totaled almost $6.8 billion, up some $340 million over 1968. It was designed to achieve and maintain prudent inventory levels in the light of operations in Southeast Asia. Over $4.7 billion was for procurement related to the war. The table below compares costs in various commodity areas over the past two years.

PROCUREMENT OF EQUIPMENT AND MISSILES, ARMY (PEMA)

(In millions of dollars)

Commodity	Fiscal year 1968	Fiscal year 1969	Percent of Change
Aircraft	962.3	660.9	−31
Aircraft spares and repair parts	300.8	154.4	−49
Missiles	455.3	843.0	+85
Missile spares and repair parts	25.1	45.0	+79
Tracked combat vehicles	409.3	285.2	−30
Weapons and other combat vehicles	195.3	223.3	+14
Tactical and support vehicles	404.7	395.9	−2
Communications and electronics equipment	603.9	623.0	+3
Other support equipment	381.4	443.2	+16
Ammunition	2,361.1	2,994.7	+25
Production base support	345.8	166.3	−52
Total	6,445.0	6,784.9	+5

Of the more than $8.2 billion in contracts awarded during the year, $6.5 billion ($5.5 from current year and $1 from prior-year funds) was for the Army and $1.7 billion for customers ordering Army equipment.

Most of the equipment and munitions delivered in the 1969 fiscal year were contracted for in 1968. The following table illustrates the growth in deliveries since 1965.

MAJOR PROCUREMENT DELIVERIES

(In millions of dollars)

	Fiscal year				
	1965	1966	1967	1968	1969
Total [1]	2,355	2,937	5,407	7,657	8,411
Firepower					
Ammunition	497	799	2,348	3,840	4,506
Missiles	451	362	392	436	542
Weapons and combat vehicles	409	322	467	498	771
Mobility					
Aircraft	290	520	687	999	903
Tactical and support vehicles	296	423	560	687	797
Communications and electronics	265	336	491	711	581
Other support equipment	147	175	462	486	311

[1] Includes reimbursable procurement for military assistance and for U.S. Navy, Marine Corps, and Air Force.

As a result of these deliveries, the estimated value of major end item assets on hand at the close of the fiscal year was $21.7 billion. The increase in requirements was largely due to support of Vietnam operations, which involved expanded use of aircraft and increased ammunition consumption for new and conventional weapons. Other factors contributing to increased requirements and high costs were the addition of temporary forces to maintain the ground defense posture, accelerated production, and inflation. Deliveries resulting from the substantial procurement funds appropriated for fiscal year 1969 and anticipated for 1970—over $11 billion in two years—will close a part of the gap between existing assets and requirements.

Support of Operations in Southeast Asia

In the four fiscal years from 1965 through 1968 the logistical base for U.S. participation in the Vietnam War was constructed, linked with the home base, placed in operation, and progressively enlarged to accommodate the expanding U.S. commitment. As the buildup leveled off in 1969, the program to equip the South Vietnamese forces to take on a larger share of the war was accelerated, while logistic planning was focused on developing an orderly schedule of actions to accompany U.S. withdrawals.

The adjustment of force levels, combined with improvements in port capacity, ship availability, and depot capability, brought an adjustment in the transportation phases of war support. In fiscal year 1969 the capability to move over 900,000 short tons of materiel and supplies per month over an 8,000-mile pipeline had been achieved, along with the capability to rotate the theater's personnel on the short tour basis.

About 50 percent of all Army-sponsored cargo and passengers moved to and from Southeast Asia during the year. The Military Sea Transportation Service moved 9,122,200 measurement tons into the area, down by 97,600 from the previous fiscal year. Cargo shipped by air totaled 221,500 short tons, up 22,900 over the previous year. Of the totals, 6,605,600 measurement tons were shipped by surface and 131,900 short tons by air from the continental United States. Over 14,000 short tons were airlifted by the Red Ball Express expedited service.

Passenger movements were both inter- and intra-theater. During the fiscal year 947,900 passengers were moved from the continental United States to support operations in Southeast Asia. Of the total, 863,700 were moved by air and 84,200 by surface; 150,400 moved within the theater.

A shallow draft port at Vinh Long became operational in February 1969, increasing to 11 the ports used by the Army in South Vietnam: Saigon, Qui Nhon, Cam Ranh Bay, Vung Tau, Vung Ro, Cat Lai–Nha Be, and Nha Trang as deep draft ports, and Dong Tam, Phan Rang, Can Tho, and Vinh Long as shallow draft ports. Port congestion is no longer a problem. The average time a deep draft ship waits for a berth in Vietnam ports has been reduced from the 20.4 days of the critical 1965 period to an average of less than 1 day. The deep draft ports have a daily "throughput" capability of 26,000 short tons. (Throughput includes a variety of factors such as berth-anchor capacity and discharge, onward movement, and destination reception capability.)

Monthly throughput—discharge and outload combined—in Army-operated ports in South Vietnam decreased by about 100,000 short tons during fiscal year 1969, the average dropping from 807,000 in the opening quarter to 728,000 in the closing quarter. The decrease is attributable primarily to reduced tonnages rather than handling capability, another reflection of the leveling-off process in the theater.

Closely allied to the transportation phase of military operations is supply support. Under current consumption factors, U.S. Army personnel in Vietnam are using an average of 94.04 pounds of supply (of all classes) per man per day, compared with 45.34 pounds during World War II in the Pacific theater.

The Army's ammunition support effort continued to expand during the fiscal year with the inclusion of ground munitions support to Republic of Korea forces in Korea, and, in Vietnam, to the Republic of Vietnam's Navy, Marines, and Air Force in addition to its Army forces. Procurement and production of Army munitions for Southeast Asia were based on continuing assessment of consumption experience and force levels to insure responsive support without overprocurement. In view of competing demands for ammunition, the Military Services Ammunition Allocation Board controlled apportionment of production deliveries among the military departments, while the Department of the Army Allocations Committee for Ammunition performed the same function for the Army. Careful and continuous monitoring of theater stocks and shipments has kept the vast majority of items at the levels required to meet combat needs.

Under the direction of the Secretary of Defense, the Army provides a limited number of administrative and general housekeeping items, packaged petroleum products, and subsistence items to all U.S. forces in the II, III, and IV Corps Tactical Zones in the Republic of Vietnam. The Navy provided similar support in the I Corps Tactical Zone. Extension of the Army common supply support system and expansion of the categories of items handled will depend upon the Army's general supply posture and further direction from the Secretary of Defense.

Combat operations have placed a heavy burden on maintenance funds and activities. The growth rate of the U.S. Army, Pacific, depot maintenance program, for example, has been almost three times the worldwide rate. To shorten the maintenance cycle, ease the transportation burden, and take advantage of favorable labor costs in the Far East, maintenance work has been done as far forward as possible. Some repairs have been undertaken in the theater that would not have been economical in the continental United States. Depot maintenance is now performed in a score of shops in Japan, Korea, Okinawa, and Taiwan, and the closed loop support program, under which critical items are withdrawn, repaired, and returned to the user, is now fully operational to support not only U.S. Army forces in Vietnam but those in Thailand, Korea, Okinawa, Alaska, and Europe. The program embraces 86 major and 93 secondary items and in the past year over 40 line items were removed from a critical supply status. The maintenance support capability in the Pacific will be highly useful when and as the war is terminated and materiel is redistributed.

As noted in last year's report, the U.S. armed forces were left with $12 billion in surplus stocks at the end of the Korean War. The high cost of identifying, processing, and storing large amounts of excess materiel, coupled with rapid deterioration and obsolescence, tends to encourage the early classification of war surpluses as salvage. To insure that such waste does not occur in Vietnam, a program has been going forward since November 1967 to identify excesses and redistribute them according to need. Of the more than $700 million worth of identified excess materiel in the Pacific by the end of the fiscal year, the Army reported assets of $515 million, with approximately $177 million of these assets having been redistributed.

The program to improve and modernize the armed forces of the Republic of Vietnam, initiated in the spring of 1968, proceeded during the fiscal year, with progress attested to by the battlefield performance of Vietnamese forces and the announcement that an initial increment of U.S. forces would be withdrawn. Force levels were increased, funds allocated, procurement initiated, and equipment delivered to augment stocks already on hand. At the year closed, the supply of the most essential weapons and combat vehicles was well in phase with Republic of Vietnam Army unit activation schedules and maintenance and attrition requirements.

Support of Operations in Europe

In the first quarter of fiscal year 1969 the major redeployment of Army troops from Germany to the United States was completed. Two brigades of the 24th Infantry Division (Mechanized), the 3d Armored Cavalry, and 78 support units were involved in the move, completed on September 30, 1968. The majority of their equipment was prepositioned in Germany against future need, and the units, although stationed in the United States, remain committed to the North Atlantic Treaty Organization and under the operational control of the Commander in Chief, U.S. Army, Europe. To test their availabiliy on call, the major 24th Division units and selected support elements were deployed by air to Germany in January 1969 to participate in Exercise Reforger I, using their prepositioned equipment.

As a part of the continuing effort to improve the U.S. logistic posture in Europe, a study was made of the management considerations connected with prepositioned materiel configured to unit sets. The appraisal addressed management procedures; funding and construction of controlled humidity storage facilities; readiness reporting; disposition of overage equipment; depot maintenance program data; and storage, maintenance, and modernization policies.

In March 1969 the Secretary of the Army approved the plan, proposed by the Commander in Chief, U.S. Army, Europe, to reorganize the logistic system in Europe, and the majority of actions embodied in it were completed in the final quarter of the fiscal year. The reorganized structure consists of a theater army support command and two corps support commands, and makes use of modern management techniques.

Under the military construction program, the Army continued to fund the United States share of the NATO common infrastructure program. The Congress authorized the $55 million budget request, but appropriated only $47 million. The other NATO nations agreed to share the cost of relocating U.S. facilities from France, and reimbursements began in the fourth quarter of the fiscal year.

Materiel Maintenance

In fiscal year 1969 the Army obligated $791.8 million for depot maintenance activities. Of this amount, $550.3 million was used to overhaul, convert, renovate, modify, repair, inspect, and test materiel. The remaining $241.5 million was used to plan and program maintenance activities; provide technical and engineering services; and procure capital equipment and basic issue items. Of the grand total, $649.5 million was directly related to maintenance support of the Army buildup and operations in Southeast Asia.

Two worldwide depot maintenance programing conferences were held in the Washington, D.C., area during the fiscal year, one in December 1968 and the other in April 1969. The 1969, 1970, and 1971 fiscal year budgets were reviewed and the entire program adjusted in the light of maintenance and repair schedules, the condition of existing materiel, and projected requirements. Broad consideration and regular updating are essential to insure that the program is responsive to the heavy maintenance requirements placed on it, for the maintenance of materiel is as important to combat readiness as the procurement of new stocks.

A joint Army-industry team, established to collect and evaluate data on armored personnel carriers and tanks in Vietnam, completed its work in the report period. One result of the appraisal was to change the standard overhaul frequency schedule for the M–113 armored personnel carrier from 5,000 to 6,000 miles of operation. The extension increases the operational availability of a vehicle by 20 percent and saves millions of dollars in overhaul costs.

The Army-industry team mission has been expanded to include evaluation of data on all combat vehicles worldwide. Evaluation of autofrettage in gun tubes was begun this year, along with a program to improve the techniques by which wear-out and replacement factors for parts and components of tank retrievers are developed.

The Department of the Army prescribes standards for the operational readiness of equipment that measure both equipment and logistic support performance. The standards are considered to be attainable and are consistent with equipment distribution, geographic environment, usage, and command priorities. They have been established for each major command and separately for Vietnam and the Reserve Components. Updated readiness standards for Army ground equipment and aircraft became effective in December 1968.

Army Aircraft

Worldwide readiness standards were set in 1969 at 80 percent for fixed-wing and 75 percent for rotary-wing aircraft, with a weighted average of 76 percent for all aircraft.

Because of the large number of aircraft in Vietnam and the time required for surface transportation from the United States, air movement of both aircraft and components to the battle zone has become increasingly important. Aircraft losses must be replaced immediately, either from new production or through repair programs. Thus cargo planes—C–124, C–133, C–141—transport new aircraft and parts to Vietnam and bring back damaged or high-use aircraft for repair and overhaul in the United States. Also helpful in keeping aircraft operational is a new technique designed to diagnose an engine's condition. Called the spectrometric oil analysis program, it improves the aircraft maintenance diagnostic capability in Army units, reduces maintenance requirements, and promotes operational safety. All Army aircraft installed engines were diagnosed during the year, and the feasibility of extending the technique to ground vehicles and water aircraft is being evaluated.

In September 1968 the Army was designated the integrated weapons support manager for the UH–1 aircraft and the T–53 turbine engine, responsible for providing materiel support for all such equipment used in the military services. The Army supported the Navy and Air Force through interservice agreements for the remainder of the fiscal year, pending implementation of the new agreement early in fiscal year 1970.

Forward maintenance for aircraft in the battle zone was enhanced during the year with the development of a family of aircraft airmobile shop sets that permit integration of aircraft direct support maintenance into operational aviation units. The sets were issued to the 1st Cavalry and 101st Airborne Divisions (Airmobile) and the 1st Aviation Brigade in Vietnam, and provided repairmen with the tools and equipment to perform 80 percent of the direct support maintenance requirement.

Logistics Systems

Among numerous recommendations developed by the Department of the Army Board of Inquiry into Army Logistics Systems were those relating to improvement of the logistics systems of Army divisions. Extensive changes in the system were proposed, along with an increased use of automation. Tests were conducted at Fort Hood, Texas, and in U.S. Army, Europe, between September 1967 and August 1968, and a number of new methods were approved in such areas as management of repair parts, maintenance of the property book, asset reporting, and inventory control. Organizational realignments were also adopted that would provide more effective and efficient supply and maintenance support to the combat battalions. The changes were in progress in the 24th Infantry Division at Fort Riley, Kansas, as the year closed, and are scheduled for other divisions in the United States, Europe, and Korea.

Developmental work began in the fiscal year on an integrated facilities system (IFS) that would provide structured, accurate, and timely data on Army real property resources and programs. Such data is used in developing costs associated with various courses of action and in making decisions related to force structure, force readiness, and facilities planning and programing. The IFS will provide functional managers and commanders with data required to manage real property resources. In a related development, the stationing capability system was completed during the year. This will provide the Army with an automated system to be used in the preparation of stationing plans to support capabilities studies. One of its principal features will be the ability to determine dollar costs associated with troop stationing plans. This system will be incorporated eventually into what is called the facilities planning module of the integrated facilities system.

Under the over-all Program to Improve the Management of Army Resources (PRIMAR), a system is being developed to control supply and maintenance activities that are financed for the most part from the Army's operations and maintenance fund. The system will isolate key performance indicators, which will be used in conjunction with a simple reporting system to develop comprehensive budgets by computer, ideally in less time and with greater accuracy than has been possible in the past.

Management has become ever more intensive in military operations today. The size, complexity, and cost of operations, goods, and services have made this so. Contributing to the need for intensive management are limited budgets, competing demands, high costs, measured production, accelerated consumption, distant operations, and worldwide requirements, among other reasons. One of the key elements in intensive management is an effective reporting system, and one of the equipment areas that has required close management is that of aircraft components. An Aircraft Component Intensive Management System was instituted in February 1967, initially for T–53 and T–55 turbine engines. In 1968, 20 additional critical or high-dollar value items were added to the system. Testing was completed in September 1968, and the system has been made a permanent one. By the close of the fiscal year, 45 high-dollar aviation items had been brought under intensive management.

Those elements of logistics which directly concern materiel—requirements, assets, production engineering and facilities, supply and distribution, sales losses, research and development, funding levels—are integrated into the Army Materiel Plan. This is the basic document used to develop the procurement portion of the Five Year Defense Program, and items for the budget are selected from it. A system for the automation of the Army Materiel Plan became operational during fiscal year 1969. It is used at the commodity commands and the Major Item

Data Agency at Letterkenny Army Depot, Chambersburg, Pennsylvania. The system automates a large number of calculations required in the preparation of the Army Materiel Plan that were previously done manually. It provides more rapid access to information and response to changes in guidance and permits data to be updated monthly and retained in computerized form.

Several important concept studies of broad logistics implications were in progress during the 1969 fiscal year. One deals with the question of whether the extension of the Army Materiel Command overseas or some other method would provide the most responsive, efficient, and effective supply and maintenance support for U.S. forces in oversea areas; the study concludes that the Army Materiel Command should be responsible for requirements determination, procurement, distribution, and integrated inventory management worldwide. Decision has been deferred until communications and data processing systems that would support the over-all system are evaluated. The other study, approved in the year, examined the concepts and costs of an all-air line of communications and compared possible surface and air lines of communications in the 1970–75 time period when the Air Force C–5A transport will be available. It was concluded that all-air lines of communication are not feasible given the projected C–5A availability and problems of vulnerability in forward delivery; a mixed surface-air concept appears to be the most feasible.

Supply and Depot Management

Wartime conditions continued to complicate the management and distribution of Army materiel. The Department of the Army's Distribution-Allocation Committee continued to control the allocation of critical items of equipment to meet requirements and priorities around the world. Distribution planning was aided by the inception of an automated system to display equipment requirements, inventories, scheduled production, and anticipated losses. From this data a 2-year distribution plan is now compiled, reflecting the planned equipment status of major Army commands.

The Army Stock Fund finances much of the materiel that flows through the Army depot system. Stock fund purchase authority in fiscal year 1969 amounted to $3.7 billion to support an issue program of $4 billion. The purchase program was about 3 percent less than that of fiscal year 1968, while the issue program remained essentially unchanged. The Army continued to improve supply management and control in Southeast Asia, where demands leveled off somewhat, although there were some increases in connection with the modernization program for South Vietnamese forces.

LOGISTICS 79

The Warehousing Gross Performance Measurement System (described in the last several reports) is used to measure productivity and manpower utilization throughout the Army depot storage system. It has been implemented for both general supply and ammunition storage activities at all Army Materiel Command depots, and for general supply storage activities in Europe and the Pacific. It will be applied to ammunition storage in Europe in July 1969 and in the Pacific in January 1970. A gross performance measurement system for inventory control points will be installed in the Army on July 1, 1969. Use of the system will improve efficiency and reduce operating costs of depot storage and supply management operations in the Army.

Modernization of the depot storage system in the United States began in fiscal year 1967 as part of a $14.2 million 3-year program to equip depots with the most efficient materiel-handling systems and provide modern facilities, design capabilities, and layouts for effective storage operations. Through fiscal year 1969, $6.2 million had been spent on procurement of handling equipment and alterations to facilities, while $1.7 million was obligated for military construction under the program. If Army requests in the 1970 and 1971 budgets are approved and the modernization program is completed, depot storage operating costs will be reduced by about $3 million annually.

Depot organization as well as modernization was a subject of attention in the fiscal year. In May 1969 a revised depot organization regulation was issued to assist depot commanders around the world to establish and maintain a uniform structure. The standard organization makes more effective use of resources and takes advantage of the latest organizational experience of the Army. The advantages of uniformity are evident in some simple statistics. There were 47 Army depots and 35 depot activities in nine countries (United States, Japan, Korea, Okinawa, Thailand, Vietnam, United Kingdom, Germany, and Italy) on December 31, 1968, storing some seven million short tons of Army supplies and equipment and performing such wholesale functions as storage and warehousing, repair and rebuild, rail and motor vehicle traffic management, stock control, overhead and support functions, quality control, and property disposal, among other depot and tenant activities.

Installations

The 1969 Military Construction Authorization Act, approved in July 1968, provided $449.1 million in new funding authorization for the Army. Although the Congress approved a total funding plan of $628.1 million, a general reduction of $80 million was imposed, reducing the Army's fiscal year 1969 military construction appropriation to $548.1 million.

The $80 million reduction, made without reference to specific projects, required the Army to defer temporarily certain portions of the program. Some already-approved Southeast Asia programs were reduced and about $40 million in other projects deferred. Since deferred projects were still required, funds for projects that encountered award delays were transferred to them.

To comply with the congressional desire to reduce large unobligated balances, the Army on September 6, 1968, set March 31, 1969, as the date by which all fiscal year 1968 and prior-year funds would be obligated, and June 30, 1969, as the date when 1969 fiscal year fund obligation would be completed. The award of contracts was slowed by rising costs; in many instances, waivers of statutory cost limitation or redesign were necessary to hold contracts to authorized limits. Considerable progress was made, however, in reducing the backlog of unstarted projects, and the unobligated carryover for all work except that connected with the Safeguard system and Vietnam and Thailand was reduced by about $80 million. The reorientation of the Safeguard program and a revalidation of construction requirements in Vietnam created a reserve for future work in both areas.

The Army in fiscal year 1969 thus had available for military construction a total of $1,057.4 million, consisting of $548.1 million in current appropriations, $490 million in unobligated prior-year funds, and $19.3 million in transfers from appropriations of the Office of the Secretary of Defense. Funds for new work were available as follows:

	(In millions of dollars)
Major projects (excluding Vietnam, Thailand, and Safeguard)	403.2
Vietnam and Thailand	254.6
Safeguard (including planning)	305.0
Infrastructure	53.9
General authorization	[1] 40.7
Total	1,057.4

[1] Excludes $4.1 million advanced against fiscal year 1970 appropriations.

Obligations for major projects totaled $248.7 million in areas outside of Vietnam and Thailand and excluding Safeguard. Some $84.3 million was obligated for new work in Vietnam and Thailand, while $44.3 million was obligated for infrastructure, $26 million for Safeguard, and $31.5 million for planning, minor construction, and access roads.

Appropriations for military construction in Southeast Asia (as opposed to obligations) in fiscal year 1969 included $131.7 million in new obligation authority for construction in Vietnam and $7.5 million for construction in Thailand. The general reduction of $40 million assigned to Southeast Asia, plus a deferral of apportionment imposed by the Office of the Secretary of Defense, reduced the Vietnam and Thailand allocations to $40.5 and $4.3 respectively. New obligation authority for construction projects in the United States and other oversea areas in support of Southeast Asia operations totaled about $10.9 million. Over $1.3 billion in regular, contingency, and military assistance funds have been applied to military construction in Southeast Asia in the four fiscal years 1965–69.

The Army's military construction program consists of three basic elements: providing facilities that installations need but do not have, replacing aged and obsolete facilities, and improving and modernizing existing facilities. At the present time, the permanent assets at fixed Army installations have a total value of about $14.4 billion. If these facilities were depreciated over an average life of 50 years, it would require yearly expenditures of about $288 million to replace them on a cyclic basis. Based upon an assumed long-range permanent Army peacetime strength of 925,000, there is a facilities deficit of about $7.5 billion (excluding Safeguard construction). It is the Army's objective to invest $800 million in construction funds annually to overcome the deficit in about 10 years. By way of comparison, only $57 million was authorized and funded by Congress in fiscal year 1969 for replacement and modernization. Further progress has been deferred in favor of meeting the demands of the war.

On April 24, 1969, the Secretary of Defense announced actions to consolidate, reduce, realign, or close 36 military installations and activities in the United States. Four are under Army control. The radio receiver station at La Plata, Maryland, and the radio transmitter station at Woodbridge, Virginia, were announced for inactivation by July 1969. A NIKE site at Garfield Heights, Ohio, will be declared excess by December 1969, while research and development functions at Frankford Arsenal, Philadelphia, Pennsylvania, will be consolidated with similar activities at other installations by January 1973. These actions will result in the relocation of 72 military personnel and the elimination of 758 civilian spaces and will produce an annual saving of $14.2 million.

Approximately $1 billion was expended in fiscal year 1969 for real property maintenance activities at Army installations, equal to the previous year. Space in Army buildings decreased by over four million feet as a result of the closing of some installations. The amount of unexecuted essential maintenance and repair at year-end was estimated to be $228 million, the same as that for fiscal year 1968.

Real property maintenance in Southeast Asia was done primarily by contractors. In Vietnam, one firm with a work force of about 21,000 furnished all normal post engineer support to about 400,000 U.S. Army and allied assistance personnel at 104 locations. The same firm, with a force of about 2,800, provided the same type of services to U.S. Army forces in four areas of Thailand. Another contractor operated and maintained power ships and distribution systems at four sites in Vietnam.

The Army, through the Corps of Engineers, provided construction support to numerous agencies and projects, among them the Air Force (including its Guard and Reserve), the National Aeronautics and Space Administration, various Department of Defense agencies, the Military Assistance Program, the Agency for International Development, the Navy and Coast Guard, national cemeteries, and several foreign governments. During fiscal year 1969, Army Engineers contracted for approximately $385 million of construction for these other U.S. agencies and foreign governments.

Around the world, the Army controls 14.1 million acres of land that, with improvements constructed after initial acquisition, cost $12 billion. During the year, 71,194 acres were disposed of that, with improvements, had an original cost of $106.4 million. Disposal of an additional 5,328 acres having an original cost of $23.8 million, reported to the General Services Administration during the year, is in progress. During the period, 1,663,036 acres temporarily not required for military purposes were leased to private parties, and receipts in the amount of $6 million were deposited in the U.S. Treasury.

As real estate agent for other government agencies, the Army in fiscal year 1969 acquired 343 land tracts for the Air Force costing $5.4 million and 953 land tracts for the National Park Service costing $5.7 million. Real estate services were also furnished the National Aeronautics and Space Administration and the Atomic Energy Commission.

In December 1967 the Secretary of the Army was assigned responsibility for the homeowners assistance program, under which military or civilian employees of Department of Defense activities are provided financial assistance to reduce their losses if they are required to dispose of a home when a military installation is closed. Through June 30, 1969, 6,584 applications for assistance had been received and 1,947 applicants had been given financial assistance totaling $6.779 million. Some 786 mortgages totaling $6.296 million were assumed, while 2,010 applications were rejected.

Due to the suspension of work on the Sentinel program and the subsequent redirection to Safeguard, major installation redesign became necessary. The changes were required by revised assessments of the threat, modifications to technical and tactical criteria, and transfers of site locations, and the principal ones concerned power requirements, the number of radar faces, the size of the missile site radar building, the launch cell design, and the number of missiles deployed at sites. The architect-engineer contracts for the major facilities—two radars and two power plants—are being revised and design of the first sites should be completed by January 1970.

Transportation

In fiscal year 1969 the amount of Army cargo and numbers of Army passengers moved varied slightly from fiscal year 1968. The Military Sea Transportation Service moved 96 percent of the cargo that was shipped—18,901,600 measurement tons, about 65,100 less than the previous year's quantity. The Army also shipped about 318,800 short tons by air, somewhat over the 1968 level.

Passenger movement continued to reflect the policy of using the most expeditious means to move personnel and save man-days of travel. During the year, 1,698,100 Army-sponsored passengers were transported worldwide, 1,590,600 by air and 107,500 by sea. The ratio of passengers using airlift increased along with the number of passengers moved.

Restraint in the use of premium cargo transportation was also maintained through the year under the airlift challenge program, which provides for automatic review, screening, and challenge of requests initiated by field commands. An average of over 2,000 shipments per month was diverted from airlift to sealift, at an estimated cost avoidance of about $12 million per month. The diversions were made without detriment to delivery dates.

There were further refinements and improvements in the Military Standard Transportation and Movement Procedures (MILSTAMP) program during the year. The most significant concerned improvements in the procedures for moving dangerous and hazardous cargo by ocean carrier.

The safe shipment of conventional explosives, nuclear weapons, and chemical agents is a matter of continuing concern to the Army. In the field of transportation safety there were several developments during the year. Escort responsibilities for nuclear weapons were transferred from the Continental Army Command to the Army Materiel Command, and installation commanders were authorized to grant refuge, in case of need, to shipments of military explosives or hazardous materiels covered by a government bill of landing.

The proposed plan to move obsolete and unserviceable chemical munitions from the Rocky Mountain Arsenal and other installations by rail to the east coast for disposal at sea came to public attention through congressional interest. As a result of public discussion over potential hazards, shipment was halted until the National Academy of Sciences could study the matter and make recommendations. The academy determined that the most appropriate disposal procedure would be to defuse the explosive devices and detoxify the chemicals in the gas bombs, and suggested that this method be considered for all materiel scheduled for disposal. Should this prove to be impractical because of preparations already made for the disposal at sea, the academy indicated that the original Army plan be carried out. As the year closed, the Department of Defense was evaluating the academy's recommendations and disposal plans were being revised. Decision on disposition of the obsolete stock was in abeyance.

The Army's containerization program moved forward during the fiscal year. In November 1968, contracts were let for the purchase of 2,000 containers, 8'x8'x20' in size (to be called MILVANS), and 1,750 matching chassis. Initial deliveries began in May 1969. Meanwhile, a pilot operation was developed, based on the initial procurement of containers and chassis, to test the possibilities of an Army-owned MILVAN fleet.

The Army has long studied the methods and means by which to cross water, which often proves to be a formidable obstacle in military operations. The roles and missions that might be assigned to transhydro craft in the 1975–85 decade were the subject of a study plan prepared during the fiscal year by the Combat Developments Command. For study purposes, transhydro craft were considered to include those which float on the surface, those supported by air cushion or foils, and those that fly over water. In May 1969 a steering committee met to consider the study plan against the possibility that approval would permit initiation of the study in the first quarter of fiscal year 1970.

The Defense Appropriation Authorization Act for fiscal year 1969 (Public Law 90–500) restricts the purchase of buses from foreign manufacturers primarily for reasons of economy and the national interest. The restrictions apply whether the buses are purchased, rented, or leased for transportation services. To comply with the new provisions, buses of foreign manufacture used by the Army will be replaced by U.S. equipment.

The extensive requirement for lighterage in Southeast Asia has practically depleted the Army's supply of landing craft. Except for 40 LCM–8 craft received through new procurement in 1967, those now in the Army supply system were procured in the 1950–52 period. They are becoming increasingly difficult to repair and provide with spare parts. Landing craft in Vietnam have had minimum maintenance and hard use in both supply and tactical operations. In view of their importance in the logistical chain, the Army is presently preparing a procurement plan for the Five Year Procurement Program.

Support Services

Although the various types of Army support services are often considered to be routine, the fact that they deal with essentials makes them interesting, and especially so during wartime. The sheer magnitude is illustrated by the fact that the Army, during fiscal year 1969, had 4,471 troop dining facilities in operation worldwide, backed by 26 central meat-processing facilities, 12 central pastry facilities, 16 garrison bread bakeries, and many additional field facilities. There were also 153 commissary stores serving Army families worldwide, with annual sales in excess of $535 million; 112 issue commissaries supplied troop messes with subsistence valued at over $508 million.

A cumulative total of 1,138,951 interments have been made in the 85 national cemeteries under Army jurisdiction, 39,811 of them during fiscal year 1969; 2,080 of these are Vietnam casualties. Among the 85 cemeteries administered by the Army, 55 have gravesites available, while 30 others have space only for Vietnam casualties, previously reserved gravesites, or second interments in existing graves under the single gravesite policy.

The 90th Congress failed to complete action on the proposal that the National Cemetery System be transferred to the Veterans Administration. The legislation was introduced once again as the 91st Congress reconvened in January 1969.

Work continued during the year on the expansion and improvement of Arlington National Cemetery. Contracts have been awarded for a visitor center and parking lot, remedial landscaping, the development of 80 acres of additional burial area, and a water distribution system for the entire cemetery. The permanent lighting system for the Tomb of the Unknown Soldier and facade of the Memorial Amphitheater was completed in March 1969, a contribution of the American Legion on its 50th anniversary. President Nixon presided at the dedication ceremony in Washington, D.C.

The 1970 budget contains a request for $258,000 as the federal government's share of costs associated with construction work at the Arlington Cemetery gravesite of the late Senator Robert F. Kennedy. The Kennedy family will assume the cost—about $419,200—for construction of the gravesite memorial.

During the fiscal year, excess property of various kinds and in various locations at home and overseas, with an acquisition cost of $1.5 billion, was available for disposition by Army property disposal activities—by redistribution, transfer, donation, sale, or other authorized action, depending upon the nature of the property. Usable property that cost $238 million and 420,000 short tons of scrap were sold; proceeds amounted to $53 million, as against $29 million for operating the disposal program. Stocks of usable property eligible for disposal increased during the year from $375 million to $502 million. Most of the increase is at Army depots in the United States and comprises returns from Southeast Asia, disposal of stocks resulting from refinements in the supply system, and munitions stocks awaiting disposal.

VIII. Research and Development

The Army's research and development mission extends from basic and applied research to a comprehensive developmental program. Broad exploratory efforts in scientific and engineering fields are applied to the design, development, testing, evaluation, and standardization of a multitude of products and techniques that have military applications. In fiscal year 1969 this over-all task was shaped by the immediate demands of the war in Vietnam and the long-range programs that advance and secure Army capabilities against future need.

Funding

The Army's research and development program for fiscal year 1969, initially established at $1,661.9 million, was conducted at a level of $1,678 million, approximately the same as that for previous years. A major portion of ballistic missile defense research performed by the Advanced Research Projects Agency (ARPA) on Project Defender was transferred to the Army (see below). During the year it was necessary to obtain additional funds to accelerate research and development that supports Southeast Asia operations. Emergency fund requests submitted to the Office of the Secretary of Defense totaled $55.2 million; $39.6 million of this amount was provided. In summary, at the end of the fiscal year, the research and development program of $1,678 million was financed as shown below.

FUNDING OF ARMY R&D PROGRAM, FISCAL YEAR 1969

(In millions of dollars)

New appropriations	1, 522. 7
Recoupment from prior year accounts	79. 3
Procurements from OSD emergency funds	39. 6
Transferral from ARPA	37. 9
Transferred to Army National Guard	−1. 5
Total	1, 678. 0

Mobility

The Army has initiated two aircraft development programs considered vital to the expanding role of aviation in the Army combat team. These programs, the heavy lift helicopter (HLH) and the utility tactical transport aircraft system (UTTAS), are designed to develop new aircraft systems for introduction into the inventory during the period 1975–80. Both are now in the concept formulation phase, in which a written requirement is defined. The HLH program will provide an external load capability for tactical airlift of the majority of the Army's combat vehicles, including the mechanized infantry combat vehicle (see below). The UTTAS program will produce an aircraft to replace the battle-proven UH-1 series. In UTTAS development, emphasis has been placed on improving the maintainability, reliability, and survivability of the assault vehicle, while increasing the troop lift capability to a complete squad plus three crew members.

The AH-56A Cheyenne, an integrated aerial weapons system, was specifically designed to provide the Army with a heavily armed high-speed helicopter to escort airmobile forces and provide direct fire support. A computerized continuous solution fire control and navigation system plus night vision devices will make the Cheyenne the most effective attack helicopter in existence. The production contract was canceled during the fiscal year because of technical problems. The development program is still in effect, however, and an early solution to technical problems is expected. There are no firm plans to enter into another production contract at this time.

Test operations with the six U.S. pilot models of the main battle tank (MBT-70) built in the United States and the six built by the Federal Republic of Germany under the joint development program have continued in both countries as component designs are confirmed or refined. The deliberate pace of this program is intended to field a joint tank that will be not only more effective but more durable and reliable than present standard vehicles.

Efforts to increase the mobility of lightly armored vehicles continued with the completion of concept formulation for the armored reconnaissance scout vehicle (ARSV) XM-800 and the mechanized infantry combat vehicle (MICV) XM-723. These vehicles, successors to the M-114 command and reconnaissance vehicle and the M-113 armored personnel carrier, will provide increased firepower as well as mobility. The ARSV will incorporate new electro-optical sensors to provide an improved capability for armored cavalry units to locate enemy forces, while the MICV will give the infantry a vastly improved capability of fighting while mounted.

Firepower

Development of TOW and DRAGON, complementary heavy and medium antitank weapons, was highlighted by the first manned test flights and successful engagement of moving targets with DRAGON and award of contracts for limited production of TOW. No significant technical problems have been encountered in the progress of DRAGON, while TOW's engineering and service testing program revealed reliability and accuracy exceeding that originally predicted by the Army. The fielding of TOW will enable the infantry to engage and destroy the heaviest known enemy tanks at ranges equal to or greater than the effective ranges of an enemy's guns. The DRAGON will be the Army's first guided missile system powerful enough to destroy the heaviest enemy tanks yet light enough to be carried and fired by one man. Its light weight (29 pounds) and simplicity of operation will permit rapid employment in all types of terrain.

Continuing effort is being directed toward providing major improvements in artillery weapons and ammunition. Rocket-assisted projectiles which further increase range capabilities are under development for the 105-mm., 155-mm., and 8-inch howitzers.

In 1968 a comprehensive review was made of the total artillery fuze effort to identify imbalances and establish a fully integrated program. Current developments in the fields of electronic and mechanical time fuzes are designed to provide items with greater accuracy, higher reliability, and improved adaptability under adverse storage conditions. Other major objectives of the program are to reduce cost and develop fuzes that are more easily produced. It is a regrettable fact that, except for missile and nuclear weapon fuzing, the Army's current line of fuzes reflects only marginal technological improvement over the course of some 20 to 30 years. The current effort is designed to exploit the latest advances made by industry and the Army's own arsenals to develop a new family of artillery fuzes.

Concept formulation for a new rapid fire automatic cannon, known as Bushmaster, was completed preparatory to entering contract definition. This weapon will provide increased firepower for new combat vehicles such as the armored reconnaissance scout vehicle and the mechanized infantry combat vehicle.

A multiple artillery rocket system is currently in the planning phase. Five contractors are performing conceptual studies to identify design and technical approaches to an indirect fire support system that could deliver a high volume of fire rapidly on a target. Such a system would be especially well suited for use against enemy mechanized formations concentrated for limited time periods.

Development of an extended-range LANCE missile has continued. Technical problems with the feed system have been solved, and a new engine design that will provide the increased range has been approved and tested. At the end of fiscal year 1969, the LANCE missile development program was on schedule.

The Army small arms program (ARSAP) encompasses all weapons of caliber .60 or smaller, plus shotguns and infantry grenade launchers. Tasks are divided into short-range, mid-range, and long-range categories. The ARSAP was created so that the research, development, and product improvement in this weaponry would be more visible. Because of high-level interest and the newness of the project, ARSAP has undergone a number of critical reviews and analyses at various levels, including one by the recently activated Army Small Arms Systems Agency (USASASA), which has the responsibility, equivalent to a project manager, for small arms research and development, including weapons and ammunition. These reviews have improved program management.

Advanced Ballistic Missile Defense Program

At the time the Sentinel system was started in 1967, two other important but less well-known decisions were made. Concurrently they had a heavy impact on the NIKE–X advanced development program, now called the Advanced Ballistic Missile Defense Program (BMD). First, it was decided to keep the advanced research and development effort separate from the BMD deployment effort. Second, it was decided to transfer a substantial portion of the advanced development portion of ARPA's Project Defender to the Army. To accommodate these increased responsibilities in advanced research and development the U.S. Army Advanced Ballistic Missile Defense Agency (ABMDA) was established as a class II activity under the Chief of Research and Development, Department of the Army.

There are two major operating arms of ABMDA: the headquarters, located in Washington, D.C., and a Huntsville, Alabama, office. ABMDA provides the advanced technical development to support the Army in fulfilling its mission of providing defense against ballistic missile attack.

The ABMDA missions are as follows: (1) perform advanced development necessary to counter the Soviet threat to U.S. strategic offense forces and their control and communications centers; (2) perform advanced BMD developments leading to new system concepts and components which can result in significant improvement in the state of BMD effectiveness; (3) develop system responses and technology to counter a sophisticated urban threat from the Soviets or a future threat from the Chinese Communists; and (4) utilize experimental facilities to assist the evaluation of the U.S. strategic offense forces through acquisition of field data from their re-entry and penetration systems tests. To insure that adequate attention is given to each area, the ABMDA technology developments are divided according to the technical requirements of each component—radar systems, missile development, optical systems, data processing, advanced systems, discrimination technology, re-entry physics, and nuclear effects.

The Safeguard System Office (SAFSO) and ABMDA have distinct but interrelated research and development programs. The Army Safeguard organization maintains a substantial research and development effort required to complete development of the components selected for deployment in the presently defined phased Safeguard program. The ABMDA program is structured to perform the advanced development required to achieve a variety of defense system responses to a spectrum of possible ballistic missile threats. The component techniques and system concepts being developed by ABMDA are necessary to assure that options are available for the decision-makers in the event that they are required to upgrade the Safeguard system in the face of an increased threat.

In summary, the Advanced Ballistic Missile Defense Program provides decision-makers with options for ballistic missile defense. It develops advanced technology so that lead time to deployment can be minimized, schedules can be developed with confidence, and costs predicted with accuracy. It insures that technology and components are available to counter threats.

Surveillance, Target Acquisition, and Night Observation

During the past five years, major advances have been made in the technology of night vision. A significant capability was added to the Army forces in Vietnam when the first generation of image intensification devices was introduced early in 1966. In 1969, the feasibility of obtaining production quantities of a second generation image intensifier tube was established. Devices using these new tubes will be tested in 1970, and are scheduled for production in fiscal year 1972.

During fiscal year 1970 the Army will conduct extensive troop tests and combat evaluations of a combat surveillance and target acquisition system using standard night vision equipment, 11 new night vision devices developed under an accelerated research and development program, ground-based and airborne surveillance radars, and sensors. These tests will provide information on the best methods of employment of these devices and on the optimum density of issue. Additionally, any shortcomings noted will assist in guiding future research and development efforts.

The detection and location of enemy weapons, mortars, rockets, and artillery have been pursued by continued development in radar and sound ranging. Feasibility studies and development of an electronic scanning pencil-beam antenna as a counterbattery radar are nearing completion, and military potential tests of various sound-ranging sets are being conducted to determine a fieldable system.

The Army has developed and is evaluating a lightweight (12 pounds) ground surveillance radar for use by troops in forward area combat zones under conditions of poor visibility and bad weather. The system is a moving-target-indicating radar that can be transported and operated by one man and is well suited for perimeter defense of small units or patrols. To improve the detection and location of attacking enemy troops in dense jungle, a foliage-penetrating radar is being developed to provide a 360-degree coverage for base camps and airfields in jungle areas.

Army development of a visual airborne target locator system (VATLS) is nearing completion. This system, consisting of a ground and airborne station, provides the Army with the capability of locating targets with sufficient accuracy to permit first-round fire-for-effect artillery fire. The results of the recently completed 1-year operational evaluation in South Vietnam are being analyzed to determine future program direction.

Experience with unattended ground sensors indicates that this area offers considerable potential for surveillance and target acquisition. The Army is continuing to explore the various detection modes and the data collection effort that must complement the use of unattended ground sensors. Their use will be closely integrated with other means.

Communications

The division-level random access discrete address communications system (RADA) described in earlier reports has continued on schedule. During the past year, three advanced development models of the subscriber unit and one model of the automatic retransmission unit were successfully demonstrated. Additional advanced development models are being procured in order to conduct a military potential test of the RADA system in late 1970. Factors will be evaluated which relate to the capability of the applied RADA techniques to satisfy the operational communication requirements for which the system is being developed.

Project Mallard, a joint U.S. and international co-operative program to develop a secure tactical communications system, proceeded on schedule. During 1969 three major contractual system design studies were completed and were evaluated by the International System Selection Board, which includes representatives from Australia, Canada, the United Kingdom, and the United States. The results and recommendations of this board now form the proposed Mallard system design which will be further studied in phase II of the program, scheduled to begin on July 1, 1969.

The tactical multichannel communications system consists of command and area signal centers, interconnected by multichannel equipment, which permit several simultaneous transmissions over a single path.

The equipment used in this system is also used to provide non-Defense Communications System transmissions in the theater army area. Shortages of multichannel communications equipment still exist in all major commands except U.S. Army, Vietnam. In 1967, equipment utilizing a digital technique was supplied to U.S. Army forces in Vietnam. This digital equipment is being procured under a program called the Army area communications system (AACOMS). AACOMS equipment, in addition to higher reliability, is easier to operate and maintain and more responsive to the commander in terms of installation time and communications capacity.

Antimine Warfare

The countermine problem in Vietnam is a preoccupation in the developmental field because of the impact of Viet Cong mine and booby trap efforts on U.S. operations. One-third of personnel and two-thirds of vehicle losses are attributed to enemy mines and booby traps. The countermine development program is concentrating on clearance, detection, and protection capabilities. Special emphasis is being applied to Viet Cong weaponry and tactics as identified in a study and evaluation of countermine activities report, prepared in September 1968 by an Army working group in Vietnam.

Major developments include mine-clearing rollers; metal-detecting radars; a variety of metallic and nonmetallic detectors including the soon-to-be-standard AN/PRS–7 nonmetallic mine detector; mine-detecting dogs; armor kits and fire suppression systems; and artillery anti-dud devices. Developments initiated two years ago have progressed to the point where some equipment is ready to be fielded and some field tested; 17 items are scheduled for shipment to Vietnam in the next 12 months.

Space Activities

The tactical satellite communications program (TACSATCOM) is proceeding under the guidance of the TACSATCOM Executive Steering Group, established under a triservice charter. Three satellites have been launched to date: the Lincoln experimental satellite No. 5 (LES–5) in July 1967; the Lincoln experimental satellite No. 6 (LES–6) in September 1968; and the tactical communications satellite No. 1 (TACSATCOM 1) in February 1969. The LES–5 provides both SHF (super high frequency) and an ultra-high frequency (UHF) relay capability; the LES–6 features improvements such as higher power and increased band width on a circularly polarized antenna.

U.S. testing of the first two satellites has been completed. The TACSATCOM 1 satellite is currently being tested by agencies of the four military services, in conjunction with Army tests of two families of UHF-SHF ground terminals to include manpacks, team packs, and vehicle-mounted terminals. Testing is scheduled to continue for 10 months. All tests to date have been successful beyond expectations.

The Army is responsible for certain phases of the Defense satellite communications project, which aims at developing reliable, secure, and survivable communications to meet national defense needs. Both space and surface activities are included, and the Army's role is concerned chiefly with the testing and evaluation of new ground terminals, as mentioned above in connection with the TACSATCOM program. The Army is currently engaged in phase II of the Defense satellite program, which involves the development of new heavy, medium, and light terminals to use with new higher power satellites.

Recent analyses of navigation requirements and available technology indicate that a navigation satellite (NAVSAT) may offer operational and cost advantages over other navigation and position location systems. A 4-service steering group has been established to co-ordinate the joint NAVSAT research and development program; in fiscal year 1969 the Army provided the chairman for this group. Spaceborne navigation aids will become increasingly important in the future, and the Army has a need for a highly accurate and reliable all-weather positioning system for air, sea, and ground operations. A wide military user base is foreseen for satellite positioning systems, which give promise of meeting the Army's needs for timeliness and accuracy.

In addition to the various satellite programs, the Army continued to support NASA in a wide range of activities. Major efforts took place in five areas—major construction; host base support; mapping, charting, and geodesy; supporting research and technology; and other support. In the area of major construction, the U.S. Army Corps of Engineers provided design, engineering, real estate management, and acquisition support throughout the CONUS base of the NASA program, with major efforts at the Kennedy Space Center and the Electronics Research Center. Host base support, provided primarily by the Army Materiel Command, consisted of operation and maintenance of facilities and supply and services. Mapping, charting, and geodesy support, provided by the Army Topographic Command, consisted of production, reduction, and analysis of lunar orbiter data; development of an improved lunar geodetic system; preparation of photomosaics and topographic maps and relief models of the moon; and design and preparation of lunar and earth landmark graphics for use in the Apollo command module to support navigation. Supporting research and technology by the Army Materiel Command consisted of a diverse range of test programs, the use of research facilities, and studies. The Army Topographic Command conducted technical and scientific investigations on the use of lunar photography. In the area of other support, technical advisers, library services, communications, and minor construction support were provided to NASA. As of December 31, 1968, 79 Army officers were on duty with NASA.

Medical Research and Development

There have been numerous advances in medical research and development during the past year. Dermatology research, for example, has significantly contributed to the reduction of skin disease casualties in Vietnam. One year ago skin diseases were so severe as to incapacitate up to 40 percent of the maneuver battalion strength in some units. The daily prophylactic use of griseofulvin tablets has reduced the incidence of fungus skin disease from 36 percent to 6 percent of exposed personnel. Recognition and definition of "tropical ulcers" as combined streptococcal and staphylococcal infections have altered the mode of therapy and reduced the average man-days lost from 11 to 5 for such patients.

Nutrition research has clarified the precise daily requirements for Vitamin C and delineated body turnover times, specific biochemical utilization, and body storage and depletion factors.

Environmental medicine research has defined the energy cost of load carriage on head, back, hands, and feet, and thus exposed the physiological trade-offs required for various proposed new systems of load carriage. Studies of the effect of heat rash on the ability of the body to perform effectively in hot environments while the sweat glands are nonfunctional have shown that heat illness can occur up to four weeks after the clinical healing of a heat rash. This information will make it possible to predict those soldiers whose return to full duty should be delayed, lest they become heat exhaustion casualties.

In the area of surgical research, studies were continued on the effects of trauma and its treatment to improve the care of wounded soldiers; an electrical anesthesia device, which is capable of achieving a surgical level of anesthesia within three minutes and which permits recovery within two minutes of termination, has been evaluated in monkeys, and will be examined in humans once its safety has been established in primates. The blood research program continued, with the aim of revealing the metabolic reactions responsible for prolonging red cell survival and maintaining function during storage. It has been found that adenine and inosine added to the preservative solution double the survival time of red blood cells. The dependence of oxygen transport by the blood on the presence of an enzyme has been established and its relation to various metabolic pathways has been studied.

The clinical use of sulfamylon continued to confirm the findings of earlier investigative work, proving its effectiveness in the treatment of burns and demonstrating that it is responsible for the progressive decrease in major burn mortality. And the expanding bioengineering program, which is concerned with the improvement of existing blood oxygenators, upon which the oxygenation of blood is dependent, was advanced when it was determined that a fourfold increase in oxygen transfer efficiency through membranes is made possible by the use of an oscillating coil membrane. Investigations are proceeding to determine the ideal membrane surface, that is, the surface which will be least damaging to the blood.

In preventive medicine research, advances in immunology included establishment of the differentiation between early (19S) and late (7S) globulins, elucidation of cholera antibody distribution among the different immunoglobulin classes, amino acid analysis of adenovirus, and the development of a unifying concept in immunopathological disorders; the discovery of five more serotypes of scrub typhus in Vietnam; the preparation of a mouse animal model for melioidosis in order to study optimum antibiotic treatment regimens; the development of new immunofluorescent techniques for diagnosis of certain rickettsial diseases; the genetic mapping of *Escherichia coli;* and the induction of nonpathogenic organisms which are immunogenic against shigella pathogens.

Accomplishments in communicable disease research included the continued evaluation of a live oral adenovirus type-4 vaccine at many basic combat training centers; further development of the *Mycoplasma pneumoniae* vaccine; study of influenza virus antigenic shifts; study of the use of adjuvants with presently used influenza vaccines; study of the duration of immunity from tetanus and diphtheria vaccines with consideration of extending the interval between booster doses; investigation of the role of *Neisseria meningitidis* protoplasts in the pathogenesis of meningococcal disease; and development and testing of an improved plague vaccine.

Studies in aviation medicine research included in-flight cardiovascular patterns of Army aviators; exploration of characteristics of the human head and neck at the time of impact; measurement of toxic contaminants in aircraft cockpits; conspicuity of aircraft, aircraft noise, and vibration; effects of rotating environments; work on performance predictors; and work on adaptation and instrument perception in darkness.

Geographic spread of drug resistant malaria continues to occur. Recent progress in the search for effective antimalarials includes a new quinoline-methanol effective in preliminary trials against chloroquine resistant falciparum malaria. Approximately 1,000 compounds are screened weekly for antimalarial activity. Sophisticated screening techniques now permit utilization of mosquitoes, infected with human malaria, in an effort to determine which compounds are effective against the tissue stages of malaria infection. Another new screen determines the prophylactic value of drugs. Supporting research continues to concentrate on methods for studying human malaria in monkeys, and developing in vitro techniques of parasite cultivation. Other efforts focus on vaccine development and studies on the molecular biology of the host parasite relationship. Despite these efforts malarial parasites are developing increasing resistance to antimalarials, posing problems for both military and civilian populations. Further research to develop new drugs and other methods of malaria control is essential.

Biomedical stress research continued to emphasize studies with practical application to problems affecting performance and military psychiatry. Previous programs have continued, with the notable addition of the computer assistance for military psychiatry (COMPSY) project at the Walter Reed General Hospital, Washington, D.C. COMPSY will provide on-line, real-time computer support to psychiatric services within Army hospitals and mental health consultation divisions, and will facilitate record keeping, nursing notes of patients on wards, psychological testing, and patient care in general by providing accurate and timely information. Considerable progress has been made in the past year in automating nursing notes and psychological tests.

Dental research has shown that silicone rubber can be used to restore maxillofacial, soft tissue, avulsive wounds temporarily. An intraoral bandage of acrylate amide sponge has been developed and is now in a clinical testing stage. Isobutyl cyanoacrylate has been successfully used as hemostatic agent in intraoral periodontal surgery. A new material and technique now allow molding of a splint for mandibular fracture fixation directly against the mandible. A new intraoral open reduction procedure for mandibular fractures is faster, less traumatic, and reduces hospitalization time when compared with current procedures.

In the field of veterinary medicine, the Biological Sensor Department, Walter Reed Institute of Research, U.S. Army Research and Development Command, has been conducting a Biological Sensor System program in an effort to identify the most efficient breed of dog for military purposes. The activity became operational at its permanent site at the Edgewood Arsenal, Maryland, in September 1968, and research to date has included experiments to determine the feasibility of using field dogs (pointers) for off-leash detection purposes.

A major milestone of the radiation protection program was passed during fiscal year 1969 when compound No. 638, the thiophosphate derivative of mercaptoethylamine, was tested for clinical tolerance in humans. This is the first compound synthesized in this program to be clinically tested in humans since the project was started in 1959. This compound was found to be nontoxic when administered orally to volunteers, with doses in excess of 11 grams per day per individual. This experiment demonstrates that the toxicity noted in animals tends to be duplicated in humans, since the compound was found to be nontoxic in monkeys at the same dose level.

In the field of biomedical engineering and development of medical materiel, a feasibility model of the field medical laboratory was fabricated and preparations initiated for professional evaluation of this system. The study of sterilization has reviewed the state-of-the-art and has identified requirements in both materiel and techniques. Progress is continuing on the development of an automated scanner for panographic dental X rays. A study was initiated to determine the feasibility of developing an automatic fabricator for spectacle lenses.

Development continued on such field items as insect and rodent control equipment, lightweight kits and equipment for use by Special Forces, and vastly improved field dental equipment. Future projects will include studies and equipment development in automation of laboratory procedures, clinical data gathering, monitoring of patients, and patient records.

Final mobility and environmental testing of the inflatable and expandable shelters and utility element of the transportable medical unit (MUST) is being conducted by the U.S. Army Test and Evaluation Command prior to standardization. Testing has been completed on the pharmacy, dental, and X-ray units, and continues on the food service and water and waste management systems. System testing of various configurations of the surgical hospital (mobile Army) was conducted during the latter part of the year, permitting evaluation of the merits of different layouts of the hospital, the advantages of various combinations in interconnecting shelters and passageways, and employment of utility elements. The MUST hospital was also subjected to environmental testing during this period. Shelters and equipment were exposed to prolonged high humidity to demonstrate their durability under tropical conditions, and to extremely low temperatures to determine their ability to withstand service in Arctic regions.

Other Significant Research Activities

At the request of the Humble Oil Company, at least one and possibly four members of the scientific staff of the Cold Regions Research and Engineering Laboratory will accompany the ice-reinforced 1,000-foot tanker *Manhattan* as ice specialists on a Northwest Passage cruise this summer. These specialists will participate in the cruise and assemble data that will be correlated with simultaneously gathered ship structural and operational data, to be used by the Humble Oil Company as part of a feasibility study of the Northwest Passage as a year-round transportation route from the recently discovered oil field near Prudhoe Bay on the north coast of Alaska to east coast ports in the continental United

States. This work will be conducted by the laboratory for Humble Oil Company on a reimbursable basis. The cruise is scheduled to depart Philadelphia on July 15 and will last approximately three months.

A laser safety team has been established at Frankford Arsenal, Pennsylvania, where the Army Medical Research and Development Command and the Army Materiel Command are conducting a joint effort to obtain data essential to the safe field employment of existing and proposed Army laser devices and systems. Research will be conducted on the laser biological damage mechanism, hazards will be assessed and safety data generated and protective devices will be evaluated.

Research is also being carried on in the field of transparent armor. The most effective armor material thus far developed is a composite consisting of a boron carbide ceramic material with glass reinforced plastic backup plate. Transparent plastic glass laminates have now been developed which weigh less than 10 pounds per square foot and provide the same protection as the 30-pound-per-square-foot World War II laminated glass armor. Recent research has indicated that transparent armor approaching the effectiveness of present opaque ceramics is possible, and mass production of large-size transparent ceramics is under way. One objective of this effort is to provide canopies for Army helicopters that would be transparent and stop .30- and .50-caliber armor-piercing projectiles.

There are many requirements for computers to store data on a permanent basis, and the most appropriate computer storage device is a read-only memory. Classical examples of read-only memory are punched cards and magnetic tape transports which utilize special techniques to insure that permanent data is not inadvertently rewritten. Recent experiments have been undertaken in the field of holography, since holograms fulfill the important requirements of removability, high packing density, low cost, and high speed. Furthermore, holograms are immune to dust particles, scratches, and other degrading characteristics which produce erroneous information. In order to develop a degree of practical experience with holographic read-only memory as well as verification of theoretical results, the Army Electronics Command at Fort Monmouth, New Jersey, initiated construction and then evaluated a feasibility model. The first operating holographic read-only memory model, it was awarded a prize as one of the 100 most significant new technical achievements of the year by Industrial Research, Inc., in October 1968.

The Fort Monmouth group has also pioneered in developing high energy density zinc-air batteries. These new batteries provide longer service life, high reliability, and increased peak power levels for manpack electronic equipment. The zinc-air battery assembly is mechanically rechargeable, via replacement anodes which eliminate the burdensome recharging operation. The first such batteries were distributed in Vietnam in 1968 for field evaluation. The development of these greatly improved batteries represents an intimate utilization of technology from many sources, stimulated by intergovernmental co-ordination and funding.

IX. Civil Works and Military Engineering

The Army's engineering mission combines broad responsibilities in both civil and military areas, including water resources development, flood control, navigation, shore protection, real estate management, construction, utilities operation, mapping and geodesy, combat support, and emergency operations. In fiscal year 1969 the over-all engineering responsibility was shaped in immediate terms by natural disasters and wartime urgencies, and in long-range terms by the requirement to sustain and advance all evolutionary engineering activities and programs.

Civil Works

The necessity for providing urban and agricultural areas of the country with adequate flood protection was dramatically illustrated in the spring of 1969 when the winter's near-record snowfall in areas of New England, the upper Midwest, and the western mountains began to melt. Snowpack in New England and the mountain areas contained up to 4.5 times the normal average of water for that time of year.

The Weather Bureau called attention to the flood potential in early February, warning that the Mississippi River could crest higher than the record level of 1965. On February 20 the Army Corps of Engineers, which performs emergency flood control functions, began surveys to evaluate the flood potential and initiate emergency steps. Nine days later President Nixon ordered federal agencies to undertake all feasible flood prevention preparations in the northern and western parts of the country. The program, the first mobilization of federal efforts in advance of a potential national disaster, was co-ordinated by the Director of the Office of Emergency Preparedness and christened Operation Foresight.

The Army Corps of Engineers began a massive program of assistance to state and local governments. More than 400 communities in 26 states were aided with construction, supplies, and equipment. Over 320 construction contracts, valued at $9.6 million and involving the use of some 3,600 pieces of heavy construction equipment, were negotiated to build, raise, or strengthen over 200 miles of levee, break up ice and log jams, and clear channels. Nearly 10 million sandbags, hundreds of pumps, and many miles of polyethylene sheeting were provided. Over 2,000 Army employees, military and civilian, participated.

Operation Foresight proved to be highly successful, preventing an estimated $200 million in flood damage. Also significant were the many large upstream reservoirs on the main stem of the Missouri River and in the Kansas River Basin which the Army has constructed over the years as part of the nation's extensive flood control program. On this occasion, these reservoirs averted substantial additional damage.

Since 1936 the Army Corps of Engineers has completed over 650 flood control projects. The 900 corps projects of all categories now effective for flood control have prevented well over $17 billion in damages since 1918. In addition to the many major reservoir projects, 77 projects, or 28 percent of the entire specifically authorized construction program of the corps, were under way during fiscal year 1969 to provide flood protection to local communities. Many small projects not authorized by specific legislation were also constructed.

Wise use of the flood plains supplements construction in reducing flood damage. Under the Flood Plain Management Services program, the Secretary of the Army, through the Corps of Engineers, is authorized to compile and disseminate information on flood hazards and to respond to requests for technical advice and guidance in flood plain land use planning.

Through fiscal year 1969 over 300 flood plain information and special flood hazard reports were issued. Responses were made to some 2,000 requests for at-site flood hazard information during the year. In the long run this program, along with the corps' survey program and programs of other agencies, is expected to provide information on flood hazards in 7,500 communities. Planning—with flood hazard information as a basis, and incorporating flood plain regulation, flood-proofing techniques, and other adjustments, as well as flood control—is continuing at an increased pace. Several states have adopted flood plain information reports in land use planning and regulation studies.

The federal program to improve rivers and harbors for navigation, now in its 144th year, was the first water resource development activity assigned to the Corps of Engineers. The program consists of three major elements—coastal harbors and channels, Great Lakes harbors and channels, and inland and intracoastal waterways. Each of these systems has more than justified construction and operating costs by savings in transportation costs. For example, the federal government has improved in varying degrees some 22,000 miles of inland and intracoastal waterways, of which about 19,000 miles are currently in commercial use. Latest available statistics indicate that foreign and domestic traffic on inland waterways increased nearly 6.1 percent during calendar year 1967, to establish a new record of 174.6 billion ton-miles.

In addition to providing flood control and aiding navigation, a great number of the corps' projects also generate hydroelectric power. In fiscal year 1969, 1,235,000 kilowatts of generating capacity were placed in commercial operation. At the end of the fiscal year, a total of 10,875,400 kilowatts of generating capacity was in operation at 49 projects located in 20 states, representing 3.6 percent of total generating capacity and 20 percent of the hydroelectric generating capacity in the nation.

The civil works program has contributed to the nation's outdoor recreation opportunities by regulating downstream flow and creating vast expanses of water areas with thousands of miles of new shoreline. With these resources the public is able to enjoy many types of water-oriented outdoor recreation.

Over 227 million people visited Corps of Engineers reservoirs and other water project areas during calendar year 1968. An equal number are estimated to have visited the remaining unreported waterways and harbor projects. Lake Sidney Lanier in Georgia is now nearing the 10 million mark in attendance. The general policy in the past with respect to the installation of recreation facilities has been that the federal government supplies the basic requirements for public recreation, health, and safety. As a co-operative venture, many of the states and local governmental agencies participate in the funding, construction, and maintenance of public-use facilities at the corps' projects.

In November 1966, the Secretary of the Army requested the Corps of Engineers to develop a $38 million 5-year program of federal construction of recreational facilities at public access areas to encourage states and local authorities to assume operational and maintenance responsibilities for recreational areas at the corps' reservoir projects. The total program includes development of 68 public access areas on 30 projects. Fiscal year 1969 marked the initiation of the program, with the allocation of $5,074,000 for basic construction at 20 public recreation access areas located at 17 reservoirs.

Planning

During the fiscal year the Army continued its activities as a member of the Federal Water Resources Council, with the Corps of Engineers participating directly in the activities of the Council of Representatives and the various supporting technical committees and work groups. The Department of the Army contributed to the council's recently published first national assessment of "The Nation's Water Resources" and assisted in the compilation of the 1969 national water resources development map.

The Army also continued its participation in the council's nationwide program of comprehensive river basin water resources development studies. The Corps of Engineers furnished members to the interagency co-ordinating committees and commissions established by the council to co-ordinate federal, state, and local planning for comprehensive river basin development. The river basin program consists of 20 framework studies and 16 detailed type-2 studies; 7 more of the latter are under consideration. Eleven framework studies are now in progress, and four type-2 studies have been completed by the field-level co-ordinating committees. The reports submitted by the committees contain recommendations for needed water and related land resource development to meet the needs of both the near and distant future.

The Corps of Engineers is preparing a comprehensive plan to develop the water and related land resources of the Appalachian region, encompassing parts of 12 states and all of West Virginia. In accordance with federal legislation, the plan is being co-ordinated with other development programs to stimulate economic growth over a large section of the country.

As a result of the government-wide planning, programing, and budgeting system (PPB), the Army Corps of Engineers has adopted a regional approach to multiyear investment planning. Nineteen program categories have been established for PPB purposes, consistent with regional boundaries defined by the Water Resources Council. The regions are then broken down into river basins—131 in all. For each river basin, needs are then projected for urban flood damage reduction, rural flood damage reduction, water supply, commercial fisheries, recreation, navigation, and hydroelectric power.

The character and intensity of water resources problems and opportunities vary significantly among the major regions of the nation. Consequently, resource development needs and opportunities must be measured not only in physical terms but also in relation to the region's level of economic development and its concerns for environmental restoration or preservation.

During fiscal year 1969, primary attention was focused on refining estimates of need and on improving methods of program formulation to reveal more clearly the impact of alternative objectives. After extensive analysis, a 5-year water resources investment program, responsive to varying regional requirements, was submitted for consideration by the administration. Work continues on improving the PPB data base and determining survey investigation priorities to insure the timely response of civil works activities to emerging needs.

The importance of community relations in civil works planning is recognized in a study initiated by the Corps of Engineers in 1968. Designed to develop ways of improving the means of public communication and promoting local leadership involvement, a program was adopted as part of the Susquehanna River survey by the federal-state co-ordinating committee. In this area during the year, leading individuals and institutions interested in resource planning were identified; personal and questionnaire interviews were conducted; and information workshops and forums were held throughout the Susquehanna Basin to inform local and regional planners of alternatives considered in the Susquehanna survey and to identify public preferences for alternatives. Audience reactions at the meetings were recorded and are being reflected in plan modifications as the survey progresses. Additionally, a formal contributing report from the University of Michigan is anticipated in the fall of 1969.

Legislation

Development of 73 flood control, navigation, water conservation, and other water resources projects at an estimated federal cost of $1.2 billion was authorized by the Omnibus Rivers and Harbors, Flood Control, and River Basin Monetary Authorization Act of 1968. The work, to be performed under the direction of the Secretary of the Army and under the supervision of the Chief of Engineers, consists of 41 flood control and multiple-purpose projects at an estimated federal cost of $875.6 million; 31 navigation projects at a cost of $324.5 million; and 1 beach erosion project at a cost of $680,000. The act also authorizes eight surveys for flood control and three for navigation and beach erosion, and provides increased authorizations totaling $469 million for 13 river basins.

Additional general authorities are also provided by the act. The Chief of Engineers is authorized to spend up to $1 million for a 3-year investigation of erosion along all shorelines of the United States and to recommend remedial action where necessary. Investigation and construction of projects to prevent or mitigate shore damages attributable to federal navigation works is also authorized. Under the provisions of the act, the Secretary of the Army is directed to perform 1-year studies on the need for a co-ordinated program for streambank protection and removal of debris from public harbors.

The act also provides authority for the federal acquisition and conveyance to state or local entities of land for resettlement of persons displaced by authorized water resources projects. It authorizes maintenance of river and harbor projects in excess of authorized project depths where such excess depths have been provided for defense purposes and the essential needs of commerce. Reimbursement for advance work done in the public interest by nonfederal public entities on authorized projects is also authorized.

Title XIII of the Housing and Urban Development Act of 1968 authorized establishment of a national program of flood insurance covering loss or damage to real and personal property, with program priority to small residential and business property. The act authorized the Secretary of the Army to assist the administrator of the program, the

Secretary of Housing and Urban Development, to identify within 5 years all flood plain and coastal areas with special flood hazards, to establish within 15 years the flood risk zones in such areas, and to estimate flood loss rates in each zone.

Construction and Operations

The impact of expenditure limitations on the civil works program during fiscal year 1969 was severe and required centralized control over all proposed advertisements and contract awards during the period November 1968 through June 1969. The civil works expenditure ceiling is shown below.

CIVIL WORKS EXPENDITURE CEILING FOR FISCAL YEAR 1969

(In millions of dollars)

Total ceiling	1, 235. 100
Less estimated collections	—23. 238
Total	1, 211. 862

The total represented a reduction of approximately $70 million from requirements estimates in January. This reduction was accomplished for the most part by deferring contract awards and by limiting obligations on existing contracts essentially to those made prior to November. The limitations on obligations resulted in the issuance of out-of-funds notices on many contracts, but most contractors continued work with their own financing. As the fiscal year closed, the Army was able to provide some relief to these contractors within the expenditure ceiling where funds were already available for the affected projects. Where funds were not available, the Department of the Army planned to make payments to the contractors immediately after the start of the new fiscal year.

Construction activities were performed on more than 250 specifically authorized navigation, flood control, and multiple-purpose projects during the fiscal year. Construction on the $1.2 billion multiple-purpose plan for the Arkansas River and its tributaries in Arkansas and Oklahoma continued on schedule. Six of the 17 locks and dams are operational and the 9-foot channel from the Mississippi River to Little Rock, Arkansas, is open to navigation. Navigation is scheduled to be opened to Fort Smith, Arkansas, in calendar year 1969, and to Tulsa, Oklahoma, in 1970, for a total distance of 443 miles. In addition to opening a large portion of the landlocked interior of the Southwest to year-round water transportation, the project will provide flood control, produce hydroelectric power, permit low-flow regulation, and furnish opportunities for outdoor recreation. The total estimated cost of work along the navigable reach is $910 million, including $133 million for bank stabilization and channel rectification.

The project to modernize the Ohio River to accommodate the longer and larger tows of today and tomorrow is well along. The 1910–29 vintage locks and dams are being replaced by 19 gated dams with dual-lock chambers at an estimated federal cost of $1.34 billion. The improved efficiency of the new locks will permit faster lockages, and the increased size will greatly reduce the need for multiple lockages of individual tows. Six units are in operation and seven under construction.

The Ouachita-Black River navigation modernization project will provide an all-year 9-foot navigation channel extending 380 miles from the Old River, Louisiana, channel connection with the Mississippi River, to Camden, Arkansas. Six obsolete locks and dams of the existing 6.5-foot channel will be replaced by four new ones. Construction of the downstream segment in Louisiana is on schedule and expected to be open to navigation in 1971. Total federal construction cost is estimated at $97 million.

Construction of a new replacement for the 1896 Poe Lock on the St. Mary's River, a connecting link between Lakes Superior and Huron, at a total federal cost of $34.9 million, was substantially completed. The lock was opened to navigation in October 1968. Construction continued on the 107-mile Cross-Florida Barge Canal, which will provide a connecting link between the Gulf Intracoastal Waterway and the Atlantic Intracoastal Waterway across northeastern Florida. The project is about 27 percent complete.

Dworshak Reservoir, an important project in the Columbia River Basin, is 38 percent complete. Scheduled for storage and power generation in November 1972, it will also provide flood control and navigation and recreation benefits. At 723 feet, this will be the highest concrete gravity dam in the United States. The estimated total cost for the project is $252 million.

Another important multiple-purpose project in the Columbia River Basin is Libby Dam on the Kootenai River in Montana, which will provide benefits in flood control, power production, recreation, and fish and wildlife enhancement. Relocations necessitated by the project include 60 miles of railway, a 7-mile railway tunnel, and 118 miles of roads and highways. The project is 38 percent complete. Construction cost for the completed project is estimated at $375 million.

Ice Harbor, one of the four dams with navigation locks on the Lower Snake River, has been completed, with Lower Monumental, Little Goose, and Lower Granite still under construction. Benefits from the projects will include slackwater navigation through a succession of reservoirs, hydroelectric power generation, irrigation, and recreation. Lower Granite Lock and Dam is scheduled for completion in June 1975. Current estimated cost for the four is $682 million, including proposed additional units at Ice Harbor estimated at $22 million.

Research and Development

Civil works research and development activities directly support the Corps of Engineers nationwide program of water and related land resources development, which is growing in scope and complexity. Activities are aimed at developing improved methods for planning river basin development; better usage of hydrologic data in the planning, design, and operation of water control projects; improvements in engineering design and materials, as well as construction, operation, and maintenance techniques; solution of operational problems involving water quality and usage, aquatic plant control, and effects of water control structures on fish, wildlife, and other ecological and environmental values; and improvement of coastal engineering technology for the protection of coastal and Great Lakes beaches, shores, and shore structures.

Civil works research and development, which amounted to about $9.5 million in fiscal year 1969, is an integral component of the over-all federal programs of water resources and marine sciences (including coastal engineering) research and development, upon which increased emphasis is being placed.

Achievements in civil works research, and the benefits derived therefrom, have been compiled in a report published in December 1968 and entitled "Research for Civil Works—A Progress Report." Objectives of the study were to establish the monetary return on the research effort, identify future research needs, and review the scope of problems encountered in conserving and utilizing the nation's water resources.

Over the 10-year period from 1956 to 1965, a total of $126 million was saved in design, construction, and maintenance costs, whereas research expenditures for that same period totaled approximately $26 million. The savings estimate was based upon analyses of actual or estimated costs of parts of projects before and after the research findings were utilized. Less tangible benefits, such as more refined designs which lead to assurances of improved safety, were impractical to establish and thus not included in the monetary evaluation.

Conservation

Increasing concern for the preservation and enhancement of the natural environment is reflected in all phases of water resources development—planning, design, construction, operation, and maintenance. The Chief of Engineers has issued guidelines, regulations, and criteria concerning aesthetic values and environmental quality for consideration and incorporation in all corps planning and construction programs. When the national interest requires development, provisions are made for preserving natural beauty. Although this usually means mitigation measures, aesthetics may in some cases be made part of the project. For example,

Libby Dam on the Kootenai River in Montana was designed to fit the natural landscape and present a pleasing appearance. And the site of the Red River Reservoir in Kentucky was moved five miles downstream in response to the wishes of the public to preserve the intangible aesthetic values of a 2-mile stretch of the Red River Gorge. Although the alternative location requires a longer dam and the acquisition of more privately owned land, it provides approximately the same tangible benefits for flood control, water supply, water quality control, and fish and wildlife.

Planting trees and seedlings is a general practice at corps projects which contributes to scenic beauty and comfort, reduces soil erosion, dampens noise, and creates a wind barrier. Other beautification measures include screening hurricane barrier dikes in urban areas with trees, planning landscapes, banking soil along channels, aligning channels and floodways to preserve adjacent vegetation and scenery, and clearing reservoir pool areas to avoid unsightly exposure of dead trees.

An engineering and architectural achievements awards program recognizes outstanding accomplishments in architecture, landscape architecture, engineering design, and the conservation of natural beauty in corps projects. Rodman Reservoir on the Cross-Florida Barge Canal won first place for conservation of natural beauty in the landscape architectural design awards competition. Honorable mention went to Hogback Island Recreation Area, Sacramento River Bank Protection Project, Isleton, California. Receiving an honorable mention award for urban landscape design was the flood control channel improvements on Sand Creek, Newton, Kansas. John Day Dam on the Columbia River was awarded first place in the engineering design competition. The new Poe Lock, Saulte Ste. Marie, Michigan, and the Findley highway bridge, Shelbyville Reservoir Project, Shelbyville, Illinois, received honorable mention.

In addition to the close attention paid by the Army to the preservation of the natural environment in the water resources development program, planning for the proper use of natural resources on Army installations is being emphasized. Land, forest, and wildlife management plans include development of proposed recreational projects, preservation of wildlife, and retention or restoration of natural beauty with landscape plantings and other vegetative covers. The Army-wide conservation program is applied over approximately 12 million acres, of which 285,500 are improved grounds, areas that receive intensive turf grass management for dust and erosion control to provide lawns for builtup areas, and turf for drill fields, aircraft landing fields, and athletic facilities. Other areas are managed and maintained in accordance with the requirements of the military mission.

During the past year progress was made in developing adequate technical direction over the forest management program, and active fish and wildlife programs were operated at 110 Army installations under co-operative plans with the Department of the Interior and state fish and game agencies.

Pollution Abatement

The problem of water pollution has involved the Corps of Engineers in a wide variety of water quality control activities, including controlling and policing waste disposal in navigable waterways, controlling and reducing pollution originating on corps-owned lands, providing treatment facilities for the corps' floating plant, regulating streamflow for maximum water quality, developing acceptable measures for projects, and devising methods for disposal of polluted dredged material.

Sanitary and industrial wastes which have been discharged into the nation's rivers and estuaries may become a serious problem when it is necessary to dredge channels and harbors, particularly in the Great Lakes area. An extensive study of this problem in the Great Lakes area, initiated in 1966, was continued during the fiscal year to determine the best methods of disposal of polluted dredge spoil. Public meetings have been held to ascertain the public's views, and the corps will formulate its conclusions on the study during the coming fiscal year.

Water pollution control at Army installations received continuing attention in programing actions for new or expanded facilities. The Congress appropriated $4.1 million for construction of water pollution control projects in fiscal year 1969. Approximately $160,000 of operating and maintenance funds were expended in fiscal year 1969 for water pollution abatement at 15 installations.

The Army is also concerned about the problem of air pollution, and emphasis continued to be placed on control by Army installations in the past year. Most progress was made in the elimination of open burning of refuse, the procurement of fuels with lower sulfur content in order to reduce the sulfur dioxide emission from fuel-burning equipment, and the replacement of small coal-fired heating plants with gas- or oil-fired units. Approximately $3 million of operating and maintenance type and industrial process funds were expended in fiscal year 1969 for air pollution control measures in heating and boiler plants at various installations. Due to strict budgetary limitations only $1.5 million of a desired $8.4 million was appropriated by the Congress in the fiscal year 1969 military construction program.

Nuclear Energy Applications

The U.S. Army Nuclear Cratering Group is participating jointly with the Atomic Energy Commission in developing means for employing nuclear explosives on public works, and is experimenting with the use of large-yield chemical explosives for excavation. The Nuclear Cratering Group is located at the Lawrence Radiation Laboratory in Livermore, California, where it is in close contact with the scientists and engineers involved in the Atomic Energy Commission's Plowshare program. Experimental work supporting the combined effort has been conducted at Livermore, at the Nevada Test Site, and at the Fort Peck Reservoir in Montana.

Nuclear explosives appear to hold great promise for moving massive quantities of earth and rock economically. Harbor excavation is an area of special interest. To advance the knowledge of channel cutting and harbor construction by explosive means, chemical explosives experiments are continuing at Fort Peck. In fiscal year 1969 a row charge connection experiment was conducted there using seven high-explosive charges of 30 tons each, placed to connect a new row crater to one previously excavated. The resulting 50-foot-deep, 200-foot-wide section connected smoothly with the existing crater, producing an excavation more than 1,000 feet long. In the fall of 1969 that crater will be explosively connected to the Fort Peck Reservoir, creating a small boat harbor.

The results of the Fort Peck chemical explosive experiments have been very encouraging. They have produced scaling data upon which to base cratering calculations for nuclear excavation projects such as the proposed interoceanic canal. At the same time, new insight has been gained into the effects of high-order chemical explosives for construction purposes.

Turning from cratering to power applications, the United States Army barge *Sturgis,* which contains the world's first MH–1A floating nuclear power plant, was deployed during the fiscal year to the Panama Canal Zone to meet a serious electrical power shortage projected there for the next several years. The *Sturgis* uses a conventional steam-generating system to produce up to 10 million watts of electrical power to support military operations or provide electric power to communities hit by peacetime disaster.

The power shortage in the Canal Zone has resulted from a scarcity of water needed to operate the hydroelectric power plants, and increased requirements for power resulting from heavier ship traffic to Southeast Asia and the closing of the Suez Canal. The deployment of the *Sturgis* to the Canal Zone on July 26, 1968, concluded many months of engineering studies pertaining to selection of a deployment site. Close co-ordination with the State Department and the Atomic Energy Commission was required relative to political and safety requirements, and acceptance by the host government was carefully explored and assured before the *Sturgis* was deployed.

Since beginning full power operation in the Canal Zone, the *Sturgis* has been operating continuously and, by the close of the fiscal year, had produced over 40 million kilowatt hours of electrical power. To expand the Army's mobile power capability, the Corps of Engineers has initiated a cost effectiveness study to determine the most efficient and economical means of providing large blocks of electrical power to support a coastal logistical base. Other means include floating high-powered barges, both nuclear-fueled and fossil-fueled, with output capacities of 50 million watts of electrical power and 1 million gallons of desalted water per day.

In addition to the foregoing activities, the Army has continued to operate existing nuclear power plants at Fort Belvoir, Virginia, and Fort Greely, Alaska, and has provided support for the Navy's nuclear power plant in the Antarctic. Continued operation of these plants has provided invaluable data on plant and component lifetimes and reliability factors and has provided considerable operation and maintenance experience.

Although nuclear power plants are not economical at the present time for the majority of military applications, the Army will continue to develop concepts and designs for plants that meet general and special requirements and are feasible and economical.

Engineer Operations in Southeast Asia

In Vietnam the engineer force in fiscal year 1969 numbered approximately 36,000 personnel and comprised 10 percent of the total Army force. A major percentage of engineer troop activity was devoted to combat support, which reflects the continuing offensive operations by U.S. forces. Army engineer troops were responsible for more than $109 million in military construction. By the close of the year, projects totaling $107 million had been completed. In addition, $66 million in operational support, road and airfield construction, and support of the Army and other services and allied forces had been done. The Army engineer troop effort was expended during the year as follows: military construction, 34 percent; airfield and road construction, 20 percent; and combat and operational support, 46 percent.

Engineer troop efforts in Thailand have consisted of road, airfield, depot, and cantonment construction. A 41-kilometer section of highway between Korat and Kabin Buri was completed during this fiscal year. As the year closed, an engineer battalion was deployed in northeast Thailand, constructing 87 kilometers of highway to provide a supply route to the air base at Nakom Phanom. Another engineer battalion was engaged in construction of a 2,000-man cantonment for Army troops on the shore of the Gulf of Thailand midway between the new Sattahip port complex and the Utapao air base.

Research efforts with regard to the engineering needs of the Army in the field increased considerably in the past year. One development provided revetment bins five feet high and four feet thick to protect Army aircraft. Some are being used in Southeast Asia. By using bin structures, revetments can be built more quickly than by the previous sandbag method, and they offer greater protection. The development of a family of Army aircraft protection structures was also initiated. This program will recommend various structures to provide a spectrum of protection against a variety of weapons under varying conditions. The structures will range from hardened concrete facilities to airmobile frames from which fragmentation blankets will be suspended. Research is also being conducted on rapid methods of constructing field fortifications; improved ways to store fuel underground; and a system for locating buried sources of gravel by means of aerial photography.

The land-clearing equipment introduced into Vietnam in 1967 has continued to be invaluable in clearing enemy jungle havens and increasing the safety of friendly force main supply routes. The small land-clearing units were considered so important to the combat mission that a battalion-size land-clearing unit was organized during the last year for more efficient utilization of these assets. As of June 30, 1969, 333,708 acres of jungle had been cleared.

The most significant engineer construction activity in Vietnam today is the highway construction or LOC (line of communication) program. This is a concentrated military construction effort that is designed to support military operations and assist the political and economic integration of the country. It will be the focal point of the engineer construction effort in Vietnam for the next 2½ years. When completed in 1971, 4,060 kilometers of road will have been constructed or upgraded to provide South Vietnam with an all-weather, two-lane highway network.

The program has evolved from what was primarily an Army effort into what is now a multinational effort. The integration of the civil and military aspects of the program is provided by the combined Central Highways and Waterways Committee, an agency of the Vietnamese Joint General Staff. Its members include representatives from the U.S. Military Assistance Command, Vietnam; the Ministry of Public Works; the Agency for International Development; and the Vietnamese Chief of Engineers.

The objective of this year's program is to provide an all-weather road into the Mekong Delta, linking Saigon with Dalat, Phan Rang, and points north, and to push into the interior from Ninh Hoa to Ban Me Thuot. Priority of construction has been placed on Route 1 and the roadnet in the Saigon area. As of June 30, 1969, the Army had upgraded 942 kilometers of road to approved standards.

The Viet Cong and North Vietnamese have conducted nuisance mine operations in South Vietnam in increasing intensity. Army engineers have worked with tactical forces to clear many miles of communications routes on a daily basis. This time-consuming and dangerous job has not been an easy one. The nature of mine warfare is such that odds are generally in favor of the enemy forces, which can choose within wide limits the time and place of emplacement, a variety of detonating devices and techniques, and the most available type of material. During the past year additional steps have been taken to counter this enemy threat. More time is being devoted by training centers to mine warfare and to countermine and booby trap instruction with increasing concentration on Viet Cong devices. As noted in the last chapter, mine detection equipment is being improved and new models have been or soon will be sent to Vietnam. Specially trained mine detection dogs are now being used for the first time in Vietnam. Mine rollers for rapid route clearance have recently been evaluated by the Army and more are being readied for employment.

During the past year the Army recognized the need for designating responsibility for integration and co-ordination of the Army-wide mine-countermine efforts. The Office of the Chief of Engineers was designated as the Department of the Army staff agency for follow-up actions pertaining to Southeast Asia countermine activities with the added mission of co-ordinating both short- and long-term efforts to improve Army mine, booby trap, and countermine capabilities. The Army's awareness of and increased emphasis on the Viet Cong mine threat should result in an improved capability in this area.

In the last year a number of actions have been taken to improve the Army's floating and fixed bridge capabilities. Through close co-ordination with development agencies, programs that had been dormant for a considerable period of time have been revitalized.

There was a renewal of interest in a rapidly erectable float bridge known as the ribbon bridge. This system consists of integral float-deck elements that form a continuous floating runway when connected. It is designed to be erected in one-fifth the time of current comparable U.S. float bridging. Preliminary development studies have begun and a contract was awarded at the end of fiscal year 1969 for the manufacture of test sets.

Development and testing of mobile amphibious bridge-ferry (MAB) equipment also continued over the last year. Initial units were deployed to troop organizations in Europe. The MAB consists of self-propelled amphibious transporters with bridge roadway superstructures which can be easily linked together to form a continuous bridge or rafts of various sizes and capabilities. The mobility of these units and their speed of assembly will permit rapid assault river crossings in support of military operations.

Bridging developments of other nations were reviewed in an effort to improve the Army's bridging capability. The United Kingdom has developed a fixed medium girded bridge consisting of high strength aluminum alloy components that can be assembled to support class 60 loads up to 100 feet. This bridge shows great promise and is being considered for inclusion in the U.S. inventory.

Mapping and Geodesy

On September 1, 1968, the U.S. Army Topographic Command was established under the command of the Chief of Engineers. Prior to this time, Army topographic operations had been carried out by a variety of offices within the Army Staff structure. The over-all objective of the reorganization is to provide maximum readiness capabilities to satisfy Army requirements for worldwide topographic support. An effective central management structure is required to provide the best working arrangement among all decentralized production facilities and units.

In the field of geodesy, the reliance on satellites for measurements is increasing. The U.S. Army developed the sequential collation of ranges (SECOR) satellite system in 1964, and during the past year the system continued to provide support to the Department of Defense worldwide master geodetic control net. One new SECOR satellite was launched into orbit, bringing the total number to three. Much of the equipment for the SECOR tracking stations has been transistorized and is now under testing at the operational field stations.

Aerial photography has been a major component of the mapmaking process. Continued research and development has produced vastly improved optical systems both in cameras and in photogrammetric instruments. These have materially increased the speed and accuracy of mapmaking. When these improvements are coupled with computers, automated systems are the result.

A new concept—the data base and retrieval concept—envisions the establishment of a topographic data center organized to contain input data, including photography, preprocessed geodetic control data, names, and other map source information. These data would be retrieved or displayed so that they could be used in the rapid production of maps, orthophotomaps, terrain and digitized data, or other map-related products. The end products would be produced as required, thus eliminating to a large extent the need for bulk storage of maps.

Other accomplishments include progress in the field of radar mapping, initial steps toward the establishment of a military geographic intelligence base, use of the BC-4 camera in satellite triangulation, and development of an improved position and azimuth determining system for artillery survey. The new Topographic Command organization and objectives are keyed to provide progressive worldwide topographic support in this scientific and technological era.

X. Special Functions

In addition to conventional military functions, the Army is assigned certain special functions that have national implication and importance. Those related to the execution of the civil defense program have been discussed in chapter two. Other responsibilities include administration of the Ryukyu Islands and the Canal Zone government; operation of the Panama Canal; participation in certain aspects of the sea level isthmian canal investigation and study; and supervision of a national rifle practice program.

Administration of the Ryukyu Islands

The Ryukyu Islands are under U.S. jurisdiction, pursuant to the provisions of Article 3 of the Treaty of Peace with Japan. Due to the strategic location of the islands and the advantages afforded by exclusive jurisdiction, the United States has developed a most important Western Pacific base on Okinawa, the largest island in the Ryukyuan archipelago. The responsibility for administering the Ryukyus has been assigned by the President to the Secretary of Defense, who has delegated this responsibility to the Department of the Army. The governmental structure for the island group consists of a U.S. Civil Administration of the Ryukyu Islands, headed by a high commissioner who is appointed by the Secretary of Defense, and an indigenous government of the Ryukyu Islands, with legislative, executive, and judicial branches.

This was an extremely important year for the islands politically, because it saw the achievement of a long-standing Ryukyuan goal of full autonomy in the selection of the chief executive. As a result of the President's authorization under Executive Order 11395, Chobyo Yara was elected Chief Executive on November 10, 1968, by direct popular vote instead of through parliamentary election as previously. The new administration has continued to operate in the established pattern of cooperation with the American authorities in promoting the welfare and well-being of the Ryukyuan people.

Since the United States has recognized Japan's residual sovereignty over the Ryukyu Islands, the question of reversion has been a key political issue in the administration of this area. The reversion movement itself has gained momentum, in part motivated by the expectation that this long-desired objective of the Ryukyuan people would be realized at an early date. As a result, widespread interest has developed in the fundamental socio-economic issues that would be involved in reversion, such as the contribution made by the U.S. base on Okinawa to the local economy and to the security of Japan and other countries in East Asia.

The long record of co-operation on the part of the government of Japan in furthering the economic and social development of the Ryukyuan people was further enhanced by the activities of the tripartite Advisory Committee to the High Commissioner, whereby representatives of the United States, Japan, and the Ryukyus develop recommendations for bringing Ryukyuan institutions in the social and economic fields into closer identity with those in Japan proper. The advisory committee has made a number of recommendations associated with the development of practical programs in health, education, welfare, and the general economy. It is believed that these steps, coupled with others presently under consideration in related fields, will help materially in minimizing the stresses and dislocations that might arise in the Ryukyuan socio-economic structure at the time of reversion.

Increased attention also was given to improving the condition of Ryukyuan employees of the U.S. forces by increasing their wages and enlarging their fringe benefits.

October 15, 1968, marked the end of the 2-year period for settling all claims against the United States resulting from the activities of U.S. troops in the Ryukyus during the seven years of the occupation (1945–52). During those two years, payment was made to Ryukyuans for validated claims in the amount of $17,728,118.73. The total amount appropriated by Congress for this purpose was $21,040,000, and the remaining amount will not be used. Although these claims had been extinguished by the Peace Treaty of 1952, the Congress supported the Army's view as to the desirability of making appropriate payment and accordingly provided the necessary funds to settle them on an *ex gratia* basis.

Although the basic costs of running the Ryukyuan educational system are financed from Ryukyuan revenues, the U.S. government has provided expanded educational opportunities for the Ryukyuan people through a steady improvement in the physical plant of their schools, in teaching equipment, and in the quality of the teaching. U.S. funds are used to assist in the important task of improving educational facilities, and the civil administration also gives special attention to developing programs designed to raise the level of human resources in the islands and to insure the availability of trained persons to provide leadership. Substantial amounts of U.S. appropriated funds are allocated each year for the advanced education and training of many Ryukyuans, including graduate and undergraduate students, national leaders, physicians, and technical trainees. Almost all of these are sent abroad for their education or training, about half of them to the United States. Thus about 190 Ryukyuan youths studied at American universities under either full or partial scholarship grants. The program whereby the Army has for many years made available American academic personnel to advise the faculty and staff of the University of the Ryukyus was greatly broadened. Ryukyuan professors were able to undertake advanced graduate work in the United States, and American professors were sent to Okinawa to consult with their Ryukyuan colleagues on specialized fields of study.

The civil administration has made significant progress in guiding the activities of the indigenous government in the field of public health. The strides taken by the combined efforts which have been exerted in this field are indicated by the fact that malaria has virtually been eliminated and other diseases have been brought under various degrees of control. The lifespan of Ryukyuan women has advanced from 52 in 1935 to over 75 in 1968, and that of the men from 47 in 1935 to nearly 69 in 1968.

The Ryukyuan economy continued its record upsurge. The gross national product rose to $644.4 million in fiscal year 1968, an 18.7 percent increase over the previous year. Prices rose less than 5 percent, reflecting the growth in real terms as slightly better than the 13 percent recorded in the past two years.

The full amount of the new $17.5 million authorization for Ryukyuan economic aid was appropriated by the Congress for fiscal year 1969. However, $1.8 million of that amount was placed in reserve pursuant to the reduction in fiscal year 1969 appropriations under the Revenue and Expenditure Control Act of 1968.

The two largest foreign investments ever to be made on Okinawa were consummated in the fiscal year. Pacific Gulf Oil Corporation began construction of a crude oil storage terminal on Henza Island. The civil administration awarded a contract to Esso Standard (Okinawa) Ltd. on February 10, 1969, for the establishment of an 80-thousand-barrel-per-day oil refinery on Okinawa which, when completed, will be the largest industrial activity in the Ryukyus.

It was agreed at the 17th meeting of the U.S.-Japan Consultative Committee held in Tokyo on January 13, 1969, that a Japanese aid program to the Ryukyus of $63.2 million would be carried out in Japanese fiscal year 1969 (April 1, 1969–March 31, 1970). The program includes $48.5 million in grant aid and $14.7 million to be used for loans to the Ryukyuan government for industrial development and other activities. This is the second consecutive year for such loan assistance.

Administration of the Panama Canal

By authority delegated to him as the personal representative of the President, the Secretary of the Army has special responsibilities for Panama Canal matters which include operations of the Canal Zone government and Panama Canal Company. The Canal Zone government is administered under the supervision of the Secretary of the Army by the governor of the Canal Zone who is appointed by the President. Management of the Panama Canal Company is vested in a board of directors appointed by the Secretary of the Army as "stockholder," representing the interests of the United States as owner of the corporation. The Secretary of the Army serves on the board of directors and has appointed the Under Secretary of the Army as a member and chairman of the board.

In fiscal year 1969, 14,602 oceangoing ships, including 1,376 U.S. government vessels, passed through the canal. Toll revenues were approximately $96 million, which includes credits for transits of U.S. government vessels. Panama Canal revenues are applied against operating and capital expenses of the canal enterprise. Detailed financial statements are published in the annual reports of the Panama Canal Company and Canal Zone government. The toll figure for 1969 represents an increase of almost $3 million over 1968.

Interoceanic Canal Studies

Determining the feasibility of building a new sea-level canal to accommodate the increasing number and size of ships using the waterway is the task of the Atlantic-Pacific Interoceanic Canal Study Commission. The Department of the Army represents the Department of Defense on this presidential commission, with the Deputy Under Secretary of the Army for International Affairs chairing the National Defense Study Group and providing membership on the Foreign Policy, Shipping, and Finance Study Groups. The Army's Chief of Engineers acts as the engineering agent for the commission and directs the engineering feasibility portion of the commission's study. The engineer work is performed in co-ordination with the Atomic Energy Commission; the Environmental Science Services Administration; the Panama Canal Company; elements of the U.S. Forces, Southern Command; and other federal agencies.

Five alternative routes are under consideration, two for construction by conventional methods and three by a combination of conventional and nuclear excavation. During the year the data collection effort for the engineering feasibility study was completed. All field facilities used in this data collection effort have been turned over to the host country. The government of Colombia will continue to operate the Alto Curiche weather station and six of the hydrology stations on Route 25 and will furnish all collected data to the United States, contributing to a broader base of knowledge of the weather conditions in that area.

Collected data is still being evaluated; however, drafts of some portions of the final report have been prepared and are under review. This work will continue in the coming year, with the draft report scheduled for completion by July 1970. Further evaluation of the nuclear aspects of the study were aided by the Atomic Energy Commission's successful detonation of the 35-kiloton device that produced a crater approximately 850 feet in diameter and 200 feet deep.

Promotion of Rifle Practice

Because of budgetary restrictions, the Civilian Marksmanship Program during fiscal year 1969 was reoriented towards the support of junior shooters between the ages of 12 and 19 whose service obligation lies ahead of them. All support for pistol activities in the form of pistol loans and free ammunition was withdrawn; 5,000 pistols were recalled from approximately 1,100 pistol clubs. All senior clubs which did not support junior divisions were advised that they must support a junior division or their equipment would be recalled and they would be disenrolled from the Civilian Marksmanship Program. Twenty-four hundred clubs failed to meet the December 31, 1968, deadline and were given shipping instructions; by the end of fiscal year 1969 more than 10,000 rifles had been returned. The disenrollment has reduced the total number of clubs to approximately 4,733. Membership has dropped to approximately 312,292.

The civilian marksmanship sales program now allows only the sale of National Match M-1 rifles. Three hundred of these were released to qualified applicants in February 1969, resulting in a return of $45,000 to the U.S. Treasury. Army support for the 1968 National Matches was withdrawn because of budget austerity and commitments in Southeast Asia. The decision to support the matches will be made on a yearly basis.

XI. Military Assistance and Foreign Liaison

The Army's military assistance responsibility includes funding, training, logistic support, and production, while the foreign liaison function is concerned primarily with visits and accreditations.

Military Assistance

Military Assistance Program funds in fiscal year 1969 continued the rapid decline that began in 1966. The original request for fiscal year 1969 was for $420 million in new funds; this figure was ultimately reduced by the Congress to $375 million. The size of the final appropriation reflects the growing cost of the Vietnam War, the competition of domestic programs, and a certain amount of congressional opposition to the Military Assistance Program and other oversea commitments. The Army's goal is to replace grant aid with sales wherever possible, the obvious limitation being that those countries with the greatest need for assistance can least afford to pay for it.

Foreign Military Training

The foreign military training program for fiscal year 1969 exceeded $24 million for grant aid and service-funded training plus some $3.8 million for foreign military sales training. These funds supported approximately 9,100 training spaces in the United States, 8,250 spaces overseas, 66 orientation tours for senior military personnel, 35 mobile training teams, and 62 field training service personnel.

The Army training program for Vietnam continued to accelerate during fiscal year 1969, with over 951 Vietnamese receiving training in the United States. Of this number 253 were trained in engineer skills, 127 in communication techniques, and 162 in infantry-associated skills. To acquire managerial and technical proficiencies needed at home, 31 Vietnamese officers attended U.S. universities at both the graduate and undergraduate level with a view to obtaining degrees in public administration, engineering, and other career programs. In furtherance of the Republic of Vietnam Air Force improvement and modernization program, 95 Vietnamese Air Force students received rotary-wing pilot and mechanic training at U.S. Army schools. This number is expected to increase substantially during fiscal year 1970.

International Logistics

The materiel portion of the 1969 Army Military Assistance Program totaled $310 million and included varying degrees of support for 29 countries and international organizations. Grant aid recipients received $262 million in materiel, for which the Army was reimbursed, and $191 million without reimbursement during the fiscal year. Materiel delivered was predominantly from prior-year undelivered balances or from that readily available as excess to the Army's needs.

Aid to Thailand and Laos continued to require increased attention as a result of the conflict in Vietnam. Support for these countries had been transferred from the Military Assistance Program to military department appropriations in 1967, but planning, programing, and supply support remained essentially the same as under the Military Assistance Program. During fiscal year 1969, $68 million in materiel orders were received for Thailand and Laos, and deliveries of $72 million were made.

Continuous surveillance and close scrutiny have been applied to limit to the absolute minimum the gold flow resulting from the grant aid program. Foreign currencies instead of U.S. dollars were used wherever possible; offshore procurement was reduced; and oversea travel was curtailed.

To supplement the limited funds available, the Office of the Secretary of Defense, in conjunction with the Department of the Army and the other services, developed procedures whereby items not required by the military departments would be transferred to the Military Assistance Program at no cost. Although only partially implemented during fiscal year 1969, the results have been favorable. During the year, materiel valued at $134 million was transferred to military assistance recipients at no cost to their programs. A salient feature of this program is to encourage a country to accept materiel "as-is, where-is" and perform rehabilitation and pay shipping charges from its own finances. It is anticipated that, as these programs become fully operational, future year deliveries at no cost to the Military Assistance Program will be at a higher level than that achieved during fiscal year 1969.

During the year, posthostilities planning progressed to the point where a general over-all military assistance plan had been published. This subject is receiving increased attention, and emphasis is now being placed on developing detailed guidance necessary for a smooth transition to a posthostilities posture. The return of Laos and Thailand, as well as Vietnam, to Military Assistance Program funding is being studied.

The 5-year Spanish base rights agreement expired on September 26, 1968, and a new agreement was being negotiated as the year closed. The Army has actively participated in the negotiations concerning the proposed military assistance aspects of the base agreements.

As a result of various diplomatic difficulties in Peru, the U.S. military mission there was requested to leave the country. Despite the expulsion, military assistance grant aid shipments continued, and negotiations were under way to create a new complement of U.S. personnel to administer the program in Peru.

Due to increased North Korean aggression and infiltration, the supply of Army materiel for the prior and current year Korean military assistance program has been expedited, including a shipment of large numbers of individual weapons to arm the Republic of Korea Homeland Defense Reserve Forces.

Continued improvement in the economic conditions and industrial capability of some military assistance recipients has resulted in reductions in materiel support without materially affecting military posture. For example, the materiel program for the Republic of China in fiscal year 1969 is well below the levels provided just three or four years ago. Of considerable impact in this regard has been the availability of excess equipment in Southeast Asia. The Republic of China, through its U.S. military advisers, has been extremely active and effective in obtaining useful equipment from property disposal yards and other excess sources.

With regard to the foreign military sales program, fiscal year 1969 was the first year of operation under the Foreign Military Sales Act of 1968. The 1968 statute separated foreign military sales from the Foreign Assistance Act of 1961 and imposed several new restraints on the sales program. Under the provisions of the new law, the so-called revolving fund was abandoned; the Department of Defense was required to obtain from Congress each year such funds as are required to finance those foreign military credit sales for which no other credit is available. Congress also annulled the authority of the Department of Defense to guarantee Export-Import Bank credit to the less developed countries, and placed a ceiling on the foreign military sales credit program.

During the fiscal year, the Army sold materiel and services valued at $558 million to 57 countries and 4 international organizations under the foreign military sales program. Materiel thus sold ranged from the most sophisticated missile systems and Army aircraft to rifles, repair parts, and support equipment. Through accelerated management, 2,543 outstanding sales cases were balanced and closed out in supply records.

The Army's Logistical Orientation Tour Program brought nine groups of high-ranking military personnel from eight countries to the United States during the year. The purpose of these tours was to acquaint foreign personnel with new military systems and equipment of interest to them. Demonstrations of the TOW heavy antitank weapon and Hueycobra helicopter were conducted in Europe for members of the NATO community. One Chinook and one Cobra helicopter were made available to U.S. industry for demonstrations at the 1969 Paris International Aviation and Space Salon.

The Army participated in 16 coproduction programs with six foreign nations and the North Atlantic Treaty Organization. Valued at $1.4 billion, these programs will result in an expenditure of approximately $506 million in the United States for goods and services. Countries involved are the Federal Republic of Germany, Italy, the Netherlands, Norway, Japan, and the Republic of China. Items being coproduced are the M–113 armored personnel carrier, M–60 tank, UH–1D helicopter, NIKE-HAWK missile, M–109 self-propelled howitzer, wheeled vehicles, M–72 light antitank weapon, and certain small arms.

In the co-operative logistics support area, the supply support arrangement is one of the major forms of support. Under the terms of such an arrangement, the participating country is provided continuing logistic support including secondary items and repair parts required for all mutually agreed-upon end items of U.S. origin or design. The participating country deposits with the Treasurer of the United States sufficient funds to reimburse the Army for the cost of materiel to be held for the country in the Army supply system plus appropriate service charges. At the end of fiscal year 1969, the supply support arrangement program was valued at $162.8 million and involved 17 foreign countries and 1 international organization. The Army is supporting a variety of items ranging from conventional weapons, vehicles, and communication equipment to the more sophisticated missile systems such as SERGEANT, PERSHING, and HAWK.

The supply support arrangement program is basically concerned with support in peacetime. Under the terms of an addendum to the arrangement with the Federal Republic of Germany, however, the United States has agreed to provide repair parts support to Germany during an emergency period or a conflict involving NATO, as mutually agreed. The extent of this support is limited to the assets funded by Germany in peacetime and established in the U.S. supply system.

Another form of co-operative logistic support is a contractual agreement between the Army and a foreign nation to provide maintenance for specified end items and their components. During fiscal year 1969, the Army provided maintenance support and related services valued at $2 million.

In October 1968, the Office of the Secretary of Defense amplified earlier policy concerning logistic support of equipment furnished under the international logistics program. In general, the Army is responsible for insuring that plans are developed for providing support for U.S. equipment in the hands of friendly foreign countries throughout the life cycle of equipment as determined by the country. A long-range program has been established for the orderly and continuous development of support plans.

Foreign Liaison

Each year many foreign dignitaries visit the United States as guests of the Secretary of Defense, the Secretary of the Army, the Chairman of the Joint Chiefs of Staff, and the Chief of Staff of the U.S. Army. The Army's Foreign Liaison Office conducts their tours, some for "very important persons" and others connected with the Military Assistance Program. In 1969 this office supervised 21 VIP tours and 85 Military Assistance Program tours involving 1,606 allied officers. In addition, the Foreign Liaison Office arranged some 10,500 visits by foreign nationals to various U.S. military installations and commercial facilities. Approximately 3,000 written requests for information were received from foreign military attachés and processed by the office during the year. The Foreign Liaison Office also handled requests for accreditation of foreign personnel as liaison officers, exchange officers, and special project officers to Army staff sections and other activities. At the close of fiscal year 1969, approximately 530 foreign officers had received accreditation.

XII. Summary

After rising steadily over a period of four years, over-all Army strength reached a peak in fiscal year 1969 and began to drop off slightly as the year closed. The Army's commitment in Vietnam also leveled off with the arrival early in the year of the last major unit, a brigade, scheduled for deployment to the war zone. In the theater the 101st Airborne Division was converted to the airmobile configuration, the second of its type in the U.S. Army.

The year closed with a substantial reduction of Army forces in prospect, following President Nixon's announcement in June 1969 that 25,000 troops would be withdrawn from Vietnam by August. Further reductions will depend upon the level of conflict, the capability of South Vietnamese forces to replace American units, and progress in the Paris peace negotiations. Toward that end, Army efforts were accelerated during the year to train and equip South Vietnamese forces of all categories to assume an increasing share of the war, and the advisory effort was sharply expanded in support of the pacification program.

With the prospect of a gradual reduction in force in Southeast Asia, and to avoid problems that developed at the close of the Korean War, plans and programs were instituted for a phased and orderly redistribution of materiel throughout the Pacific area. Excess stocks were being identified, classified, and transferred to meet valid requirements.

In Korea and Europe, U.S. Army forces continued to help friendly nations maintain their political and territorial integrity during a period of heightened tension produced by North Korean provocation along the demilitarized zone and the Soviet invasion of Czechoslovakia.

In the United States, Strategic Army Force readiness gradually improved as the Army's strength and the Vietnam commitment leveled off. Veterans of the fighting brought their experience into the training base and the Strategic Reserve.

Although the Army, like American society, was affected by social unrest during the year, there were hopeful trends. Opposition to the establishment of missile installations quieted when the ABM system was directed along new lines, and civil disturbances involvement was far less than in the previous year. While opposition to the war continued, manifested in various forms of dissent, it is likely to proceed in direct ratio to the course of the war, and a leveling down in Vietnam will undoubtedly produce a corresponding decrease in war-related unrest.

As fiscal year 1969 closed, the general outlines of a gradual reduction in manpower, deployment, combat casualties, and expenditures were beginning to take shape. While the fiscal year 1970 strength and budget will remain roughly at 1969 levels, and while there are still such intangibles as battlefield developments and enemy intentions to consider, there is every reason to hope that the general stabilization in the Army and the war, begun in 1969, may be carried even further in the new fiscal year.

Index

Deputy Chief of Staff for Logistics: 60, 65

Desertion rates and convictions: 5, 43–44

Detroit air defenses: 30–31

Direct Mail Shelter Development System: 21

Director of Automatic Data Processing: 59

Director of Installations: 60

Directorate for Civil Disturbance Planning and Operations: 14

Directorate of Management Information Systems: 59

Disaster relief, Army role in: 14–15, 57, 100–102

Discipline, and attempts to undermine: 5, 44–45

Disease rates: 45

Dissension, fomenting: 44–45

Distinguished Service Medal awards: 35

Distribution-Allocation Committee: 78

Divisions, troop strength: 3–4. See also by type.

Doctrine, formulation of: 28–33

Dogs, research in use of: 96

Dong Tam: 72

Draft evasion. See Desertion rates and convictions; Selective Service System.

Draft Presidential Memoranda: 66–67

DRAGON medium antitank-assault weapon: 30, 87–88

Drugs, illicit use of: 40

Dworshak Reservoir: 106

Education. See Schools, civilian; Schools, military.

Educational deficiencies, waiver of: 26

Eielson Air Force Base: 12

Election campaign, 1968: 14–15

Electronics. See Communications-electronics systems.

Electronics Command: 98

Electronics Research Center: 93

Elmendorf Air Force Base: 12

Emergency Broadcast System: 22

Emergency operating centers: 21–22

Engineer Construction Advisory Detachment, 539th: 16

Engineer troops and operations: 16, 100–15

Enlisted Personnel Directorate: 38

Enlisted troops. See also Manpower.
 career options and management: 38–39
 number in service: 34
 personal data on: 39
 promotion system: 39
 recruiting and retention: 38, 41

Environmental Science Services Administration: 119

Equal opportunity and employment: 6, 49–50

Equipment stocks. See Materiel and supply.

Erosion, shoreline: 104

Esso Standard (Okinawa) Ltd.: 118

European theater. See United States Army, Europe.

Explosives, shipment of: 83–84

Export-Import Bank: 123

Facilities, construction and maintenance. See Construction programs.

Fallout, protection from: 20–21

Family Housing Division, Office of the Chief of Engineers: 60

Federal Communications Commission: 22

Federal Republic of Germany: 30, 79, 87, 124

Federal Water Resources Council: 102–03

Federal women's program: 49–50

Field Artillery Branch: 40–41

Finance Center, Army: 68

Finance Center, 44th: 68

Findley highway bridge: 108

Firepower, programs to improve: 87–89

Five Year Defense Program: 67, 77

Five Year Procurement Program: 84

Flood damage and control: 100–102, 104–05

Flood Plain Management Services: 101

Floods. See Disaster relief, Army role in.

Florida air defenses: 33

Force Accounting System: 4, 61

Force development: 24–33, 62

Forecast operation: 15

Foreign law, violations of: 44

Foreign Liaison Office: 125

Foreign military sales: 123

Foreign military training program: 121

Foresight operation: 100

www.ingramcontent.com/pod-product-compliance
Lightning Source LLC
Chambersburg PA
CBHW021337090426
42742CB00008B/638